"INCOMING,"
I SCREAMED.

➤

The pilots that hadn't awakened on the impact of the first mortar were now scurrying for their bunkers.

Up to now we had only been attacked with mortar fire. Suddenly, automatic weapons began to open up on the south edge of our camp. A ground attack was underway. Sergeant Lynn ran down to our tent to tell the standby pilots to launch their helicopters immediately. The standby helicopter and crew were assigned every evening and were to fly high over the camp, dropping flares in the event of an attack. The gunships were to launch also. As one of the gunship pilots ran from his tent, a mortar round hit the corner of the entrance just as the pilot reached the opening. The blast tore the front of the tent to shreds and hurled the pilot to the ground.

Several Viet Cong had reached the concertina wire and were trying to breach the perimeter...

➤

D0985925

WINGS FOR THE VALIANT

ROBERT W. SISK

WARNER BOOKS

A Time Warner Company

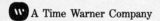

To my son Bobby, my mother Anna, and
most of all to the helicopter pilots
and crewmen who gave their all.

Robert W. Sisk

CONTENTS

1

The Decision

The one-hundred-foot boom of the big crane turned gracefully toward the steel columns. The beam dangling from the crane's load line glided along silently with the swing of the boom. The only sound was the idling engine of the crane as it eased the load into position.

Charlie Cutting sat at one end of the giant beam, I was at the opposite end. Charlie signaled the crane operator to start lifting the beam skyward.

With the finesse of a maestro conducting his orchestra, he continued to signal. With his full attention on Charlie, the operator jockeyed the levers of the crane and eased the beam into place. I quickly jammed the pointed end of a spud wrench through the bolt hole of the beam and into the hole of the steel column. Aligning the bolt holes with the wrench, I jammed a bolt into the holes and just as rapidly,

1

spun a nut onto the bolt. I signaled Charlie that my end of the beam was connected. He gave the operator a final signal and the steel beam slid smoothly into place at his end. We put several more bolts into the mated iron; tightened them down and walked the beam to the center where we disconnected the beam from the load line.

"Well, Chopper, they knocked four more of 'em down yesterday," said Charlie, as we sat down to wait for the next piece of iron to be sent up. He was referring to the four Army helicopters that had been shot down in Vietnam.

I had grown used to Charlie's good-natured kidding. He had started calling me "Chopper" several months earlier when I told him that I had passed the rugged flight physical and a battery of tests for the Army's Warrant Officer Flight Program.

It was June of 1965. We were erecting the structural iron for a new building at Hiram Walkers's distillery in Peoria, Illinois.

The American involvement in Vietnam was growing and the need for helicopter pilots was also increasing. I had been accepted for flight training and was due to leave for basic training prior to going to flight school.

Charlie and I both knew I'd end up in Vietnam. It was Charlie's way of voicing his concern for me. We were structural ironworkers, members of Local No. 112, Peoria. We had connected iron on several jobs and had worked together for several years.

As we sat talking, a U.S. Army car pulled up to the security gate. The gate guard motioned in our direction and then the car moved slowly toward us.

A recruiting sergeant stepped out of the car. Shading his eyes from the sun, he looked up toward me and shouted, "Hey, Sisk, do you want to leave for flight training earlier than we'd planned?"

"What do you mean?" I hollered back.

"I can get you into a flight school class starting in September, but you'll have to leave in a few days for basic training in order to do it."

I looked at Charlie. He saw with a puzzled look on his face. "What are you going to do?" he finally asked.

"I'm going," I replied, after a short pause. "Ok, when do I leave?" I shouted, looking back down at the sergeant.

"Next Wednesday."

The ironworkers on the ground and the crane operator had stopped and were listening to the ground-to-air conversation.

"The son-of-a-bitch is nuts," I heard one of them say.

"Be at the recruiting office, zero nine hundred, Wednesday," the sergeant said, ignoring the remark made by the ironworker.

It was Friday. I finished out the day, drew my final paycheck and quit the job.

The following Wednesday I caught the train from Peoria to Chicago. I was inducted the same day and rode another train to Louisville, Kentucky, to start my basic training at Fort Knox.

The basic training was easier than I had expected. I actually enjoyed the training and the conversion from civilian to soldier, however, my first meeting with our platoon sergeant was frightening. Sergeant King was waiting for us when we got off the buses. He said nothing. He glowered at us with contempt. We managed to fall into some sort of formation without a word being spoken. As we stood at attention, he began to stroll down the ranks, stopping every once in a while to stare into the face of one of the recruits.

Sergeant King was an ex–Korean War veteran and had just returned from a tour in Vietnam. He was the image of a perfect soldier. His uniform, boots and "Smokey the Bear" hat were immaculate. He stood about six feet, weighed about 180 and I judged his age to be around forty-two.

He stopped in front of us and looking around said, "You all look like badasses to me." He paused and continued to stare us down. "Do we have any badasses here?"

No one said anything. "Do any of you badasses think you can whip my ass?" I had seen a similar situation when I was in Navy boot camp ten years earlier. I was betting it was the same deal. In total fear, I raised my hand. If I was wrong in my evaluation, I was dead.

The sergeant looked at me in total disbelief. "Fall out soldier!" he screamed. Reluctantly, I stepped out of the ranks and stood facing the meanest looking man I'd seen in a long time. I had been in my share of fights and brawls and most of them with men much taller than I. I only stood five feet seven inches, so most taller men never concerned me too much when it came to fighting. This man frightened me, but I stood my ground. "So you think you can whip my ass, huh?" he continued to scream.

"Yes, Sergeant," I shouted back immediately.

"You sure you can whip my ass?"

"Yes, Sergeant," I shot back. I was beginning to wonder how it was going to end. Would I be sent home, a casualty who never even got to the war?

Sergeant King's voice lowered and with a much kinder tone ordered me to stand beside him. Again he screamed at the remaining recruits. "Does anyone else think they can whip my ass?" Silence. The sergeant paused a moment. "Does anyone think they can whip this man?" he shouted, pointing his thumb at me. Again silence. Another short pause. He slowly turned toward me. Oh no, I thought. I'm going to die. In a normal, friendly voice, Sergeant King said, "Well, it looks like we're the two baddest dudes here, so, that makes you the platoon guide.'' I almost fainted with relief.

The added duties helped stem my impatience to get started in flight school.

We graduated from basic in late August. I had become good friends with most of the other soldiers. A large number of them had orders for advanced infantry training. In the next several years, I would see many of these same names on the Vietnam casualty lists.

2

Flight School

Welcome to Fort Wolters. I hope the place is as friendly as the sign, I thought as I turned off U.S. 80 into the Army Post. "So this is where the Army makes helicopter pilots out of soldiers," still talking to myself.

Two weeks earlier I had graduated from basic training, taken a short leave and was now ready to see if I could produce what it took to be an Army aviator. I followed the signs until I arrived at Building 3180. "PROCESSING," said the sign hanging over the door.

I got out of the car, checked my gig line, adjusting my hat and headed for the entrance. Out front, a master sergeant had a corporal standing at attention. "What in the hell is this?" I mumbled under my breath. "An enlisted man chewing another enlisted man out."

I slipped in through the open door behind the sergeant and walked up to the counter. The PFC behind the counter took my records and without a word, started writing and filling out forms.

The corporal came in, all red-faced and shaking his head. "I don't know if I'm going to be able to hack this crap or not," he said to no one in particular.

"What was that all about?" I asked.

"I was just informed by that badass topkick that I am a warrant officer candidate and candidates don't wear stripes or brass. Hell, I've only been here fifteen minutes, how am I supposed to know that crap?"

The corporal wore the blue braid of the infantry, airborne wings, the patch of the 5th Special Forces and the renowned hat of the Green Berets.

"Hand me your records," said the PFC. "You have twenty weeks to bitch, but only one day to process," he added sarcastically.

"Real friendly place around here," I said to the corporal.

"Yeah, I just got back from 'Nam and I'm not used to this stateside bullshit. I would tell them to shove it if it wasn't for the fact that I re-upped to go to flight school."

"Well, I guess we're in the same boat," I said. "I spent three and a half years in he Navy and enlisted in the Army for the flight program. By the way, my name is Buz Sisk," I said, sticking out my hand.

"Bill Springer," said the Green Beret, as we shook hands.

"Here's your billet assignment, candidates," said the PFC. "Pick up your linen at the student supply and your flight gear at central issue," he said throwing some forms on the counter.

We walked through the door, looking cautiously for the master sergeant. "Do you need a ride or do you have a car?" I asked Springer.

"I have a car, but the 'ole lady has it up in Colorado. She's supposed to come down with the kids, after I get settled."

"We might as well go get our flight gear first. I believe the place is down by the main gate," I said.

We got into the car and headed back toward the main gate. We spotted the building and pulled into the parking lot. A half hour later, we came out loaded down with books, flight suits, helmets and other flight essentials.

After stuffing all the gear behind the seats of the Corvette, we drove slowly along the street until we found the barracks we were assigned. Our rooms were on the second floor. I hauled one load of clothes up the stairs, found my room and walked in. Another candidate was unpacking clothes and was trying to hang them in his closet in some sort of order. He turned as I dropped my duffel bag on the floor. "I guess I'm your roommate for the next five months," I said, introducing myself.

"I'm Brian Pray. I was just trying to store all this junk away the way this student guide shows it," he said, waving a pamphlet. "Hell, even the toothbrush has to lay a certain way."

I spent the rest of the day putting everything in its proper place. Pray had finished and was helping me. We just about had the display finished when a candidate stuck his head through the door opening and told us that all the drawers and shelves had to be lined with brown paper. We pulled all the clothes and articles out and started over. I was swearing; Pray went about the task in silence.

The first four weeks of pre-flight went by swiftly. "Well, tomorrow's the big day," said Pray. "We start our flight training," he added, swallowing the rest of his milk. The mess hall was bustling with candidates, some in flight suits, others in fatigues with their orange shoulder tabs on. This indicated that they had recently soloed.

"It looks like they should start us out flying the first month," I said. "I think it's a waste of time giving us that officer and gentleman training BS Hell, I don't give a damn about all that; I came into the Army to fly," I continued as I got up to leave.

The first day of flying was very tiring for me. I went into the briefing room after my first flight and flopped down on the folding steel chair. I had never flown in a helicopter prior to my first lesson. I was amazed with the machine and also very frustrated. "There isn't any way in hell I can fly a helicopter," I said to Springer. "The IP flew me out to the middle of a hundred and sixty acre field and told me to hover the helicopter. I had both hands and feet moving and almost racked our asses up." I paused to put my flight helmet into the helmet bag. "I don't know how anyone can fly one of the damned things." I was concerned about the possibility of not being able to fly the helicopter. I was sure I would end up in Vietnam stomping the rice paddies if I busted out of flight school. My concern and frustration were a little premature, however. After all it was only my first half hour lesson.

The flying sessions began to get longer. Most of us began to get the feel and knack of the helicopters. Some of the candidates began dropping out. Some of them found they didn't like flying. Others just couldn't comprehend the complicated task of operating the machine.

Candidates out of my class, 66-7, began soloing. Every day someone would get off the shuttle bus, dripping wet. This was always an indication that a candidate had just soloed. On the way back from the various stage fields, his fellow candidates would have the bus driver stop alongside one of the numerous stock ponds and they would throw the newly soloed pilot into the water. This was, traditionally, wetting down the new birdman's feathers.

More and more candidates were arriving at the school. The need for pilots had mushroomed beyond all belief. The United States' commitment to the Southeast Asian war was obvious. They began squeezing three candidates into each room. Springer moved in with Pray and me.

"Hey, bastards, I soloed today," Springer said, coming through the door wringing wet. Pray had soloed two days earlier. I still had not. "What in the hell are you waiting for, Buz, the class behind us?" Springer wanted to know.

"Go screw yourself. That IP busted me on my check ride. He said I couldn't do an autorotation good enough. Besides, maybe I don't want to get dunked in that pond full of cow piss," I said, lying back on my bunk.

My Instructor Pilot had recommended me for solo flight a week earlier. In order to solo, however, another IP had to fly with the candidate to make the final recommendation. The IP that gave me the final pre-solo checkride, was known to flunk candidates in order that his students might be the first or among the first to solo in the class.

My IP was very upset at what the other instructor had done. I had to take a couple additional pre-solo flights and then soloed a day later. The thrill of being alone in the helicopter for the first time was exciting. It also squelched my bitterness toward the unscrupulous IP who had held me back.

The barracks inspection had been slated for zero eight hundred. Pray, Springer and I had made an effort to get the room prepared for inspection, although it wasn't as spotless as most of the other candidates' rooms.

It was twenty past nine and the inspection party still hadn't shown. Pray and Springer were doing table jumps, a game we had made up. Each candidate would put both hands on the table and, without moving the hands, he would leap up on the table, coming to rest in the squatting frog position. I was stretched out on my bunk.

A sergeant came whipping into the room, hollering, "AAH-TEN-SHUN!" Pray and Springer were trying to get their jackets on and I hit my head on the upper bunk while trying to get up. A captain walked in and asked, "If it isn't asking too much, could you people tell me what in the hell is going on here?" addressing his question to Pray.

"Table jumps, Sir," Pray answered, staring straight ahead.

"Oh, that explains everything. What in the hell are table jumps?"

"Well Sir, it's an exercise we do when the weather is bad," said Pray.

"Are you people ready for inspection?" the captain bellowed.

We shouted "Yes Sir," simultaneously.

The captain started pulling razors, toothbrushes, underwear and other articles out of the drawers. The sergeant was snooping around the sink, hunting for stains. He picked up the wastepaper can that had been stored neatly under the sink. Looking inside, he let out a yelp and threw the can straight up into the air. It came clattering down onto the floor, startling the captain who was now inspecting the closets. He fell backwards, dragging Springer's clothes with him. He landed on the floor with the clothes covering him completely.

The sergeant thrust the can under Springer's nose. "What in the hell would you call that on the side of this can?"

"I would call that chili with beans, Sergeant," Springer said, unblinkingly. I had bought a can of chili out of the "gut" machine the night before. After eating the chili, I had thrown the can into the wastebasket. Some of the leftover chili had slopped down the inside of the can. I had emptied the trash can the next morning before the inspection, but had forgotten to wash and dry it out.

"What would you say it is, candidate?" said the sergeant, holding it under Pray's nose.

"I would say that is plain chili without beans, Sergeant," said Pray, staring straight ahead.

"What do you call this?" he said to me, again poking it up in my face. I looked down, made a swipe through the chili with my index finger and stuck my finger in my mouth.

"Oh, I would say it definitely is chili with beans, Sergeant," I said licking my finger.

"Stand at attention, you fucking idiot," the sergeant screamed. We could hear the other candidates in the nearby room chuckling and laughing out loud. They were enjoying the act. "I don't give a good rat's ass what it is. What in the hell is it doing there?"

We remained silent. We felt we had carried the unplanned scam too far already. The captain, shaking his head, started for the door. "I can't believe the Army needs pilots this bad," he mumbled as he left.

We received two weeks' restriction and additional duty for the inspection screw-up. A few days later, Springer's wife and family moved down from Colorado and he was authorized to move off the base to family housing. Pray and I complained. They decided to forgo our restriction and let us off the hook also.

The flight training continued at a rapid pace. We would fly a half day and then go to classes on military subjects the other half.

At nights, Pray and I would sneak off the base and go to Fort Worth, the nearest large town. One night while in a local pub in Fort Worth, we stumbled across a party in progress. They had a huge piñata dangling from the ceiling. They would blindfold a person, turn them around and let them whack away at the colored piñata.

The waitress came over to our table and dragged Pray out onto the floor. Amid his protest, she put the blindfold on him and handed him the papier mâché bat. She spun him around a couple of times and turned him loose. Pray began swinging, but every time he got close to the piñata, someone pulled the rope, raising the piñata out of reach.

Spotting a broom in the corner, I walked over, grabbed it and sneaked up behind Pray, trying to keep from getting clobbered. I grabbed him from behind and handed him the broom. I whispered to him that they kept raising the piñata and that he should reach way up and smash down real hard.

I spun him around in a circle about five times. Instead of pointing him towards the piñata, I lined him up on the bar, where several patrons were drinking, paying little attention to the festivities.

I told Pray to swing, "Now," with all his might. He belted some poor bastard on top of the head about the time he was taking a slug of beer from a bottle. The blow jammed the bottle into the customer's mouth and then slammed him face first on the bar.

Pray, thinking he had at last connected with the piñata, continued to pulverize the patron. With my encouragement, Pray bashed and destroyed everything and everyone along the bar. The waitress finally got up enough courage to slip in behind Brian and put a bear hug on him. After getting him calmed down, she pulled the blindfold off. I was in hysterics over the whole show. Pray looked around with a stunned look on his face. When he saw me laughing, he became madder than hell. The man who had gotten bashed with the broom was unwinding from his stool. He was on the verge of going berserk. Everyone else started moving slowly toward us. I broke for the doorway and went through it, only a fraction of a second behind Pray.

3

Graduation

O n the 18th of February, 1966, I completed the first phase of the Warrant Officer, Rotary Wing Aviator course. There was a graduation ceremony at Fort Wolters. We were elated to have the first part of the flight training behind us. We were given several days' travel time to reach Fort Rucker. We would be taking our instrument training and the final phase of our flight training at Rucker.

I enjoyed the trip to Fort Rucker. Stopping in Vicksburg, Mississippi, and taking a tour through the Civil War Battlefield. I stood silently in front of the various memorials, reading the names of the men who had fought and died there. I studied the Illinois Memorial a long time, searching for a person with my last name and wondering if some of my ancestors had died there.

* * *

Fort Rucker is located in southern Alabama. I checked in and was assigned a barracks and a room. We were assigned to some old barracks that had recently been reopened. They hadn't seen any use since the Korean War.

Basic instrument training began on the 1st day of March. The old feeling of apprehension came creeping back into my mind. The fear of flunking out of flight school had plagued me since the very day I was accepted for the training.

Graduating from Fort Wolters had eased the tension for a while, but starting a new phase of training at a new base, had rekindled the old feeling. Out of all the training, I thought the instrument phase would be the most troublesome. Surprisingly, the instrument course went quite well.

On the 21st of April, I passed my advanced instrument check ride. Once again I felt relief at having completed another portion of the flight training. I had but one phase to go. This was the transition into the UH-1 Bell Helicopter. In the years to come, this helicopter would become the work horse of the Vietnam War. The "Huey" as it would become known, and the pilots and soldiers it would carry into battle were destined for a place in history.

We would eventually learn gunnery, tactical flying, formation flying and external sling loads. Little did I know that in the following year, I would spend over a thousand hours of my life in the skies over Vietnam, flying the Huey.

Class 66-5, the class just ahead of us, graduated. We were now the senior class. The likelihood of becoming an Army Aviator looked ever more promising.

The closer we came to graduation day, the more talk and gossip switched to Vietnam. We were handed "Dream Sheets," a form that wanted to know where we would like to be stationed. It was a joke, because we knew most of the class would end up in 'Nam anyway. I filled the sheet out, requesting such exotic assignments as embassy duty in

Tahiti. My third request was for 1st Air Cavalry. I had no problem receiving my last choice.

We started gunship training. This was an exciting and enjoyable time. We were given instructions on the firing of the machine guns and rockets mounted on the helicopters.

A few days into the gunnery portion of our training, tragedy struck. A gunship carrying three classmates, the instructor pilot, the crewchief and a gunner, was making a down-range clearing run. The policy was to check the firing range out to see that it was clear of people and other aircraft, prior to making any live firing passes.

As the Huey gunship pulled up and started a turn, the aircraft shuddered and plunged into a heavy section of trees.

The three warrant officer candidates were killed instantly. The other crew members were critically injured.

Word of the accident spread rapidly. Our class was numb with shock. The accident brought a feeling of despair and the realization of the dangerous profession that all of us had chosen.

The loss of the three classmates was only the first of the many close friends that we would see die in the months and years to come. Death in the Vietnam War would not let our class go unscathed.

We graduated on the twenty-first of June, 1966, received the Wings of an Army Aviator and were appointed as warrant officers. That evening there was a gala graduation party. Everyone was in dress blues, sporting newly acquired wings and warrant officer epaulets. The wives and girlfriends were elegant in their evening gowns.

I was late for the party. My date lived in Troy, Alabama. By the time I drove the eighty-mile round trip, we had arrived too late to go through the reception line and protocol of the party.

I was a little uneasy as we walked into the huge ballroom.

As my girl and I stood there, the general's aide walked up and introduced himself. He escorted us over to where the Base Commander, General Tolson, and his wife were standing, and introduced us.

Less than a year later, I would again meet this fine general in a dusty little camp in Vietnam, called LZ Two Bits.

4

A Sad Farewell

We were granted a leave after completion of flight school. Everyone welcomed the opportunity to return home prior to going to Vietnam. I also dreaded the day I would have to say goodbye to my family.

Most of my leave time was spent visiting relatives and friends.

I stopped by the Ironworkers Union Hall. Walt Palmer, the Business Agent, asked if I would like to work for a few days. A new World Headquarters office building for Caterpillar Tractor Company was under construction in downtown Peoria and they needed another connector, badly.

Not having worked iron for a year, I was sluggish and slow. The second day on the job, my hand slipped while climbing a column. I almost fell. We were working at the twelfth-story level. The close call scared me. It was the closest I had ever been to falling in all the years of working as an iron worker. I worked the job for five days, until another connector was available.

In the summer of 1966, most of the major airlines were on strike. It was impossible to get a flight to the West Coast. This meant I would have to travel to Oakland, California by train, if I could get tickets. It also meant that I would have to leave home sooner, as it would take several days to travel from Chicago to Oakland.

The day of my departure arrived. I had already bid most of my relatives goodbye. My parents were going to drive me to the train. There was just one person left to say my goodbyes to.

Grandma Simms had seen one son off to war during World War II. He had been shot down twice while on bombing raids over Germany. "Gram," as she was affectionately called by all of the grandkids, knew the horrors, the frustrations and the despair of having a loved one going off to war.

I did not fear for my safety, but hated the grief I knew I would cause my family and Gram by my leaving.

She was sitting in her rocking chair on the front porch when I drove up. Her eyes were red; she had been crying. I got both of us a cup of coffee and joined her on the porch.

We talked for two hours about everything, from when I was kid, to the weekly trips to the doctor. I would pick Gram up in my Corvette and drive her to the doctor's office. She always enjoyed the kidding about having her own sports car and chauffeur.

We both avoided the topic of why I was there.

Finally it was time. "Gram, I've got to go," I said softly. "I'll write you. Don't worry about me," I added. Out of the thousands of words in the English vocabulary, it seemed this statement was the only thing people could come up with in this type of situation. It sounded stupid. There should be something more appropriate to say. I couldn't think of anything else.

I leaned over and kissed her forehead. We hugged each other. Tears ran quietly down her cheeks. I cried for the deep hurt I had just created. "I love you, Gram," I said as I turned and pushed the screen door open. "I love you too. I'll miss you," she said. On the sidewalk, I turned and waved. She waved back; her handkerchief still clutched tightly in her hand.

Somehow, we both knew we would never see each other again.

5

Welcome to Gehenna*

The big Air Force troop transport touched down gracefully on the wet runway at Pleiku. The soldiers sat silently, some of them with their faces pressed against the small oval windows trying to get a glimpse of this place called Vietnam. The C-141 turned off the runway and taxied slowly back toward the far end. The same thought popped into my mind as it had for the last year.

Did I make a mistake by enlisting in the Army? I didn't have to be here. I had fulfilled my military obligation back in '55 by joining the Navy. Now, eleven years later, I was in the Army and in a foreign country I knew nothing about except what I'd read in the papers and seen on TV.

*Any place of extreme torment or suffering.

An Air Force sergeant was opening the door; I hadn't realized the plane had stopped. Everyone remained in their seats as if waiting for someone else to make the first move. Finally the aisle began to fill as the men shuffled slowly toward the door. I worked my way into the line and slowly down the steps. I was prepared to fall on the ground if the shooting and shelling started, but was pleasantly surprised to find it quite peaceful and rather quiet. It had been raining and the air had a fresh, moist smell to it. As I looked around I could see helicopters lifting off on the far side of the airfield. Over by the edge of the aircraft parking ramp, a long line of GI's stood quietly watching as the new arrivals filed from the plane. They were in khaki uniforms with their duffel bags lying beside them. It was quite obvious that they were on their way home. I noticed that the usual smart remarks and catcalls were missing from the GI's waiting to go home. Instead they just stared at us with a tired look of pity on their faces.

They knew what we didn't, what lay in store for us for the next year. They also knew that some of us would never see home again.

Recognizing a friend getting off the C-141, a black soldier shouted, "Hey, Grady, about time you got your rump over here." Grady made his way through the crowd. They shook hands and slapped each other on the shoulder. A captain and a first sergeant in jungle fatigues drove up in a Jeep. The captain got out and walked to the newly arrived soldiers. "You men assigned to the 25th Division, grab your gear and get on those busses over there," he said, pointing to several olive drab busses. "Everyone going to the 1st Air Calvary load on those caribou," he said, motioning toward several twin engine prop planes.

I found my duffel bag and headed for the planes. An Army specialist 5 grabbed my bag and threw it in the cargo opening. Two Army warrant officers, one a W-3 and the other a W-2, were standing by the plane. They were evidently the pilots. The W-3 said, ''You fixed wing or helicopter pilot?'' as he eyed the wings on my fatigues.

''Helicopter,'' I replied.

''All nuts,'' said the W-2. ''I thought you might be my replacement. Well, you'll get plenty of flying where you're going,'' he added with a grin.

We lifted off and flew just under the low lying clouds at about three hundred feet above the ground.

I unfastened my seat belt and made my way to the hatch that lead into the cockpit. ''They've got an automatic direction finder at An Khe, but it very seldom works,'' the W-2 explained, ''so we have to go low level through Mang Yang Pass when the weather's bad.''

''That's the pass just ahead,'' said the W-3. ''That's where the Frenchies got their butts kicked back in the '50s,'' he said as he adjusted the r.p.m. on the props. I could see the rusted hulks of tanks and armored personnel carriers lying alongside the highway. The French had been ambushed and lost over two thousand men in this pass. Many of them were buried on the hill overlooking the pass.

The pilot lowered the landing gear as I walked back to my seat. We touched down and I could see mud and water kicking up from the wheels. Back in Oakland, California, I couldn't understand why they told us to change into fatigues before we left the States. As I stepped off the caribou and into the mud up to my ankles, I figured this must be one good reason.

After finding my mud-splattered duffel bag, I sloshed over where several other newly arrived pilots were standing. Almost all of them were from my flight school class. We were the replacements for the pilots who had come over with the 1st Air Calvary Division ten months earlier.

A major walked over and told us to leave our gear where it was and to follow him. He lead us to a large tent about a hundred and fifty yards west of the parking ramp. "Line up where the sign says 11th Aviation Group. You'll get your unit assignments there," he said as he turned and walked off.

After a twenty-minute wait, I was next to enter the tent. Inside, there were several soldiers busy typing and sorting papers. This struck me as humorous. It appeared to have the look of a well-organized and orderly office that could have been found at any Army post in the States. I guess the funny part was the dirt floor with little pools of rain water scattered throughout the tent.

I handed the sergeant my orders. He separated the copies and put them in different stacks. "Any particular unit you want to go to, Sir?" he asked as he handed back a copy of my orders.

"I'm not familiar with any of the outfits," I replied.

"Well, the 227th and 229th are Assault Helicopter Battalions. The 228th is the Support Battalion. They are flying the big Chinooks," said the sergeant.

"I guess the 229th will be fine," I said.

"OK," he said, starting to write. "Do you want to fly slicks or guns?"

"Who is getting the most flying time?" I asked.

"The slicks are doing more flying but if you wants lots of shoot 'em up, then the gunships are getting most of that."

"I'll fly the slicks, I want the flight time."

"All right, Alpha, Bravo or Charlie Company," he said, looking up.

Hell, I thought, I didn't know it was so damn complicated to sign up for a war. "C Company," I replied, picking the last one he had mentioned.

"As soon as I get everyone processed in I'll call the units

and someone will be down to pick you up," he said, still writing. I walked out of the tent and into a steady downpour. Officially and on paper I was in the war.

Three of us, Owens, Bair and myself were assigned to Charlie Company. The executive officer of the company picked us up in a Jeep and drove us to the company operations tent at Camp Radcliffe. The camp had been named after Major Radcliffe, an Army aviator and the first member of the Air Cavalry to die in Vietnam.

The executive officer told us that the company had just come back from a tour of duty down by Tuy Hoa. They were now responsible for perimeter patrol at Camp Radcliffe and provided the air assault helicopters for the Ready Reaction Force. They also resupplied the fire bases in the surrounding area.

Two days before Charlie Company's return to An Khe, they had lost four air crewmen in the final phase of Operation "Nathan Hale." The Huey slick had been hit with either an anti-aircraft shell or an artillery round. It literally disintegrated the helicopter, killing all on board. A memorial service was held that evening for the dead crewmen. I didn't attend; I was one of the dead pilot's replacements. I was assigned his living quarters. When I got there, some of the other pilots were clearing out his locker and putting his personal belongings in a box. One of them was crying silently. I felt real bad and scared.

The next day Captain May, the operations officer, introduced us to the company commander, Major Williams and the other pilots. I was scheduled to fly with Chief Warrant Officer Hollis Scoggins. We were to fly a training mission and then do some resupply runs to the firebases.

Scoggins requested a west departure with a right turnout. An Khe tower gave us immediate clearance for takeoff. I eased the collective up, adding left pedal to counteract the rotor torque and lifted the Huey to a hover. A quick glance at the instruments showed everything in the green. I eased the cyclic stick forward, pulled a little more collective and we moved smoothly forward with an immediate climb. We climbed to 500 feet and started a right turn.

"Turn to a heading of zero nine zero," Scoggins said. "We'll go over to Phu Cat and do some autorotations." Phu Cat was about twenty-five miles east of An Khe. We paralleled Highway 19 for a while and then the road suddenly veered southeast, dropping down into a valley.

I flew the next several days with Scoggins, learning the methods of combat flying that he and the other "first in the country" pilots had learned the hard way. Scoggins returned to the States the following week, his tour of duty completed.

6

Air Assault Into LZ Hell

O n the first day of August, 1966, the 1st Air Cavalry
joined with the 3rd Brigade, 25th Infantry Division
in Operation "Paul Revere II." The 3rd Brigade had
made contact with elements of four North Vietnamese Army
Regiments.

The operation was to be the 50th such operation for the
Air Cavalry since its arrival in Vietnam.

My company, "Charlie" or C Company, 229th Assault
Helicopters, was dispatched to Landing Zone Oasis, a
forward firebase southwest of Pleiku. Our area of operations
would cover from Pleiku to the Cambodian border, the Chu
Pong Mountains and the Ia Drang Valley. This whole area
was covered by thick, triple canopy jungle. At Oasis, the
first battalions of the 7th and 12th Cavalry plus units of the
2nd Battalion 7th Cavalry were massing for air assaults.

During our briefings, we were told that all of the landing zones would probably be "hot" and boobytrapped. The weather was exceedingly bad with torrential rains, low-lying clouds and ground fog. This was to be my first combat air assault. I was nervous but with a feeling of excitement. The door gunners were making last-minute checks on their machineguns and loading belts of ammo into the gun chutes. The infantrymen were busy writing letters and making final preparations for the air assaults. They were checking pack, cleaning weapons and hooking hand grenades to their belts.

Several landing zones were to be assaulted simultaneously. "Slicks" from the 227th and 229th Assault Helicopter Battalions were to air assault the "grunts" into the LZ's while the big Chinooks of the 228th would sling the artillery guns into place after the LZ's were secured.

We lifted off in flights of four. Once airborne, the helicopters joined up in a diamond formation. My helicopter was the tail end of the four-ship formation. Chief Warrant Officer Neil Stickney was the Aircraft Commander, I was the co-pilot. Our flight would be the second wave into the landing zone, following four "slicks" from the 1st Platoon of Charlie Company. We were to maintain a one-minute spacing between formations. Behind us were two more flights of four ships each, for a total "gaggle" of sixteen helicopters. On each side of the gaggle, a B-model Huey gunship from Delta Company flew shotgun for the assault helicopters.

The helicopters were assigned a color code with a number. They had small plates on each side for easy identification. This helped the infantrymen to find their assigned helicopter and it also determined the position in the formation that we would be flying in. Wagonwheel Six, the code name for Major Williams flying the lead ship, Yellow One. He gave orders to aircraft commanders to have their doorgunners test fire the M60 machineguns. From the open doors of the ships ahead, I could see short bursts of tracer rounds spewing from the guns. Stickney told our gunners to fire a burst. The rapid chatter of each weapon was reassuring.

"Two minutes out," the flight leader said on the UHF radio. Up ahead I could see smoke and explosions in the intended landing zone. The dark smoke and bright reddish orange flashes of the explosions were in direct contrast to the low clouds and patches of fog. Somewhere from a firebase an artillery battery was pounding the landing zone with high explosive rounds.

"Last round on the way," a voice suddenly blurted over the UHF. One ship in the flight was usually assigned to monitor the FM radio frequency of the artillery so they could advise the flight leader when the barrage was ended. The last round was a white phosphorus, nicknamed "Willie Peter."

The Willie Peter burst in the center of the clearing, billowing a cloud of thick white smoke. "One minute out," the flight leader said. Two Aerial Rocket Artillery helicopters suddenly appeared and were making a firing run down both sides of the landing zone. The ARA ships broke off the rocket runs and went into a race track holding pattern, west of the landing zone. The first wave of slicks were touching down. I could see the door gunners raking the jungle with machinegun fire. The soldiers were spilling out both sides of the helicopters and crawling for the nearest cover. The gunships had made the initial approach with the first flight, firing their machineguns and rockets. They would then swing around and escort the next flight into the landing zone. One of the gunships was fitted with a grenade launcher and I could see it firing into the tree line, looking somewhat like a fat kid spitting watermelon seeds.

"White Flight short final," the platoon leader of our

flight said. The first flight of slicks were still holding in the LZ while the grunts continued to exit. The timing of the helicopters in the LZ was critical because the following flights were on final approach.

"If they don't get the hell out of there, we'll have to make a go around," said Stickney. About then the flight on the LZ lifted slowly and began to accelerate straight ahead. I locked my shoulder harness and lowered the visor on my helmet. A few weeks earlier, another assault company had lost an aircraft due to the windshield being shot out. Neither pilot had his visor down and the shredded Plexiglas blinded both pilots. The helicopter had crashed, killing the crew chief.

"We're in contact, the LZ is hot, the LZ is hot," an excited voice suddenly blurted over the FM radio. As we touched down I could see the "grunts" lying flat behind rotting trees and giant ant hills. To the northeast of the clearing a steady steam of tracers were pouring from the dense jungle.

"We've got automatic weapon fire on the east side," the same excited voice said. "We're pinned down. Wagonwheel Six, can we get those ARA ships in here?" he asked.

"Affirmative, Blue Fox. Do you want just the east side hit?" Wagonwheel Six asked.

"Roger, for now. We've got a heavy machinegun in the northeast corner and small arms fire all along the east side," replied Blue Fox.

"White Flight is up," Stickney said, meaning all of the grunts were clear of the helicopters.

"Lifting," the platoon leader replied. All four helicopters lifted off, still in the diamond formation.

A long stream of tracers arched up at White Two, the helicopter on the right point of the diamond formation.

"We're taking a lot of fire," the aircraft commander of White Two said in a calm, matter-of-fact type voice.

"Green and red lights, go to a staggered trail formation. We've got room in the LZ to do it. It will give you better coverage," Wagonwheel Six said.

"Blue Fox, this is Black Knight Six. Do you want your reserve platoon brought in?" the battalion commander orbiting in the Command and Control helicopter asked. Normally the CC helicopter would orbit high over the LZ but because of the low clouds they had to remain low level and well off to one side of the battle.

"If we can get that heavy gun knocked out, I think we'll be OK," Blue Fox replied.

"Blue Fox, this is Hog One, we're starting our run now," the ARA flight leader said. "We've got enough fuel for about two runs apiece," he added.

"OK, concentrate on the northeast side," said Blue Fox.

White Flight made a left 180-degree turn and I could see the next flight of helicopters lifting from the Landing Zone. Streams of tracers continued to pour from the dense foliage on the east side.

The first ARA ship was just pulling up after his rocket attack on the heavy machinegun. As the helicopter broke to the right, I saw a flash of fire from the right pocket pod. Smoke was trailing from the pod and the flames were getting bigger. "We've got a pod on fire and I can't jettison it," said the pilot of Hog One. "I'm going to put it down on the LZ," he added. The ARA ship continued in a right turn. The last flight of slicks were just lifting from the LZ as the ARA on fire rolled out level and approached the Landing Zone. Suddenly the flaming rocket pod exploded. The helicopter rolled violently to the left. A large piece of the rotor blade broke off as the ARA ship went inverted. Losing its forward momentum, the aircraft plummeted straight down.

"We've bought it," the pilot of Hog One said at almost the instant the ship hit the ground. It lay partially on the LZ with the broken tailboom sticking out of the heavy jungle growth. The whole aircraft was in flames. Several soldiers were running toward the wreckage in a low crouch. They were still being fired at from the treeline. "I'm going to land," said the pilot of the other ARA ship.

"Negative, stay on station. We've got people on the ground that will get the crew out," ordered the battalion commander.

"Black Knight Six, three of the crew are dead, the fourth one was thrown clear and he's hurt real bad," said Blue Fox.

"OK, we'll get a Dustoff in there to get him out," replied Black Knight. "Also I'm going to send your reserves in. Wagonwheel Six, pick up the Ready Reaction Force at Oasis and assault them into the same landing zone," he added.

"Roger." "We can't get a Medevac helicopter right now, they are all busy," Black Knight said a minute later. "Wheel Six, can you send one of your ships in to get that crewman out?"

"Affirmative, sir. Green Four, break out of formation and do the Medevac. Keep both gunships with you."

Green Four broke from formation and made a left turn back into the landing zone. The two gunships continued to make firing runs on the east side clearing. The remaining ARA ship had knocked out the heavy machinegun and was returning to Oasis with fuel critically low.

We returned to Landing Zone Oasis and picked up the Ready Reaction Force. We air assaulted them into the same LZ, this time receiving very little ground fire.

The following morning we were completely socked in by ground fog. I had spent a miserable night trying to sleep inside the helicopter. Four crewmen could barely stretch out inside. My position was such that the continuous downpour outside found its way through the roof of the ship and into my sleeping bag.

About fourteen hundred hours, the weather broke temporarily and the 3rd Platoon of Alpha Company, 2nd Battalion 7th Cavalry was air assaulted into Landing Zone Pink. They were in heavy contact immediately with a reinforced company of North Vietnamese regulars. The twenty-six men of the 3rd Platoon were completely surrounded, plus the fog had socked the LZ in again.

At Oasis Landing Zone we were again on standby with the Infantry Ready Reaction Force. We were told to crank up and attempt an assault to help the surrounded platoon.

Yellow One, the flight leader, lifted into the fog while the other ships held on the ground. He climbed steadily through the fog bank and broke through the layer at 500 feet. One by one the helicopters climbed out through the fog and joined up with the others. We were now between two cloud layers, southwest bound. Yellow One was trying to raise the platoon under attack on the radio but couldn't make contact. Another platoon at Landing Zone Orange broke in and said they could hear us above the fog but the visibility was zero at their location. The radio operator said that they hadn't had radio contact with the 3rd Platoon in over an hour.

"I'm going to make a slow descent through the fog and see if I can get into the LZ," said the flight leader. Yellow One rolled off to the left as the rest of Yellow Flight, in an echelon right formation, continued straight ahead. Yellow One disappeared into the fog. In about two minutes he popped back and rejoined the formation. "I can't get under this crap," said the flight leader. "We'll orbit for a while and see if this stuff will move out."

In the meantime, other ground units of Alpha Company were working their way through the heavy jungle toward

Landing Zone Pink. Around seventeen-thirty, the fog thinned slightly and we were able to find the landing zone. The enemy had broken off contact after overrunning the platoon. Eighteen of the cavalrymen had been killed and the rest wounded. The survivors had played dead as the North Vietnamese stripped the soldiers of their watches, rings and billfolds. Sixteen of the enemy were found scattered around the battlefield. Later, shallow graves were found that contained several more bodies. We flew the wounded back to Pleiku and the KIA's were brought to Landing Zone Oasis.

During the next several days, we flew resupply flights in and out of the Landing Zones. The weather continued to be a problem but flying low level we would manage to get the ammo and food into the landing zones.

On the 13th of August, B-52 bombers bombed an area known to contain a large concentration of NVA. The following day we assaulted the same area, using bomb craters and blown out jungle clearings as our landing zones. Alpha Company of the 229th Assault Helicopter Battalion was to make the first flight into the LZ's. They were to provide eight ships. My company (C. Co.) was also to provide eight assault helicopters.

The landing zones were so small that no more than two helicopters could get in at one time. The approaches had to be very steep, almost vertical because of the triple canopy jungle. The first two Alpha ships started in. The landing zones had looked fairly good from a distance but now up close the pilots could see jagged stumps 20 to 30 feet tall throughout the intended landing areas. The heat and smoke of the smoldering trees added to the precarious approach. As the helicopters closed on the landing zones, they began to lose power and lift. A helicopter with maximum pitch pulled in trying to hover, will often cause the tail rotor to lose its effect and the helicopter will start spinning to the right and settling to the ground. Alpha Company lost two helicopters in the same landing zone due to this problem.

Stickney and I were told to try and get into the landing zone that the crashed helicopters were in. We made a steep approach over the trees trying to find a place where we might be able to set down. Stickney told the crewchief and gunner to notify the grunts on board that they might have to jump if we couldn't land. I looked out the right window and could see one of Alpha Company's crashed helicopters. The pilots, Joe Suarez and John Spencer, were standing beside the helicopter watching us come in over them. The other ship was behind them, lying on its right side. They hit one of the jagged trees and flipped over, throwing the infantrymen out the side door of the Huey. One man was pinned under the helicopter. Several soldiers plus the helicopter crewmen were frantically digging as jet fuel flowed from the ruptured fuel cell. Stickney tried to stop our rate of descent as a snag loomed up in front of us.

"I can't land, that snag is too damn high," Stickney said. We kept settling toward the ground as we didn't have the power to hover. "Tell them to get out," shouted Stickney. "I can't hold it!" The cavalrymen started jumping from both sides. We were still 12 to 15 feet from the ground. As the helicopter lost the weight it began to hover, the rotor blades just inches above the snag. The last grunt out the right side had tripped as he went out the door. He plunged toward a huge rock, dropping his M16 as he fell. He hit the rock and crumpled into a heap with one leg lying at at odd angle.

We pulled out of the landing zone and headed back to Landing Zone Oasis. The flight leader diverted the other helicopters to the other landing zones nearby. We picked up two chainsaws and headed back to the landing zone where they were lowered to the men on the ground. In about 15 minutes they had several snags down and a log platform made for a landing pad.

A Medevac "Dustoff" helicopter came in and picked up the injured soldiers. The man that had been pinned under the helicopter, fortunately had been pressed into the mud and only suffered a few cracked ribs. The soldier that had fallen out of our helicopter was not so lucky. He had both legs broken and was unconscious.

All during the assault and extraction of the injured and downed aircrewmen, ground fire had been light. A few shots from concealed snipers would ring out and would be answered immediately with a volley of fire from the perimeter guards.

A few miles away, Bravo Company of the 229th Assault Helicopter Battalion was air assaulting troops into a landing zone under heavy fire. They continued to fly troops into the landing zone and had one helicopter go down. Warrant Officer Allan Cox, the aircraft commander, took a round through the windshield which hit him in the head. Cox was killed instantly. He slumped over the controls and the helicopter crashed into the trees. The remaining crewmen survived the crash and made their way back to the landing zone under heavy sniper fire.

After completing our assaults, Stickney and I, along with another helicopter, were assigned the mission of flying in supplies.

The other helicopter, piloted by Stan Becker and Jim Owens, was in front of us, approaching the new landing zone. About a quarter mile from the landing zone, they suddenly began taking fire from a small clearing. I could see the tracer rounds arching toward the descending ship. Our crewchief, manning the machinegun on the left side, fired a burst into the area where the ground fire was coming from. The firing from the ground stopped temporarily. The next two trips into the landing zone were repeats of the first. On the third flight in, Becker told us to throw a smoke grenade into the area where the ground fire was coming from. He had contacted a gunship in the area and he was enroute to work the sniper over. We finished unloading the supplies, lifted out of the landing zone and started back to Oasis. Becker asked over the radio if we had thrown a red smoke grenade to mark the sniper's location. Stickney told him we had.

"Well, there's a Chinook making an approach to that location. I hope he knows that there's bad guys down there."

The Chinook with a sling load of 105mm cannon rounds was approaching the red smoke. The pilot evidently thought that our soldiers had set the smoke grenade off to mark his drop zone. He must have heard Becker on the radio because all of a sudden the helicopter shot straight up and disappeared into the low-hanging clouds. Being in the clouds, the Chinook crew would have to fly on instruments all the way back to Pleiku, the nearest air field with navigational and instrument approach facilities. It could have been fatal if the sniper had started firing into the sling load of 105mm rounds. The gunship finally arrived and fired several rockets into the jungle around the clearing. We didn't receive any more fire. Either "Charlie" was dead or he had left the area.

Just before darkness we were released from the resupply missions and headed back to Oasis to spend the night. They didn't have a field kitchen set up yet, so we had to "dine" on C rations cooked over a can filled with sand and jet fuel. It made an amazing little stove. The sand, saturated with the jet fuel drained from the sump of the helicopter would burn a long time.

Around 2100 hours, a truck drove up to our helicopter

and started loading ammunition. Captain May came over and informed us that a platoon was engaged in a firefight, and they were running low on ammo. They were somewhere east of the landing zone where the two helicopters had crashed. As I put my armor-plated chest protector on and fastened my shoulder harness I began to get an uneasy feeling. Too many things had happened today in that area. Oh well, Stickney didn't seem too concerned, I thought.

We lifted off and flew southwest. In the total darkness, we would have to fly by the time and heading to reach the landing zone. When we figured we were in the vicinity, we started calling on the FM radio to the unit on the ground. We made contact and the radio operator told us that we were a little bit south of their position. Stickney turned back to the north and a minute later the radio operator said we were right over them. We could now see tracer rounds flying in all directions. He said we wouldn't be able to land but we could get in close enough to kick the ammo out. We tried but it was so black we couldn't see the clearing.

"You will have to fire a flare so we can spot the clearing," said Stickney.

"If we fire a flare we're going to give away our position," answered the radio man. "Can't you use your landing light to spot the clearing?"

"I'm not going to use the landing light while hovering around looking for a clearing. We'll get blasted out of the sky." So far the only outside lights we had on were the standard navigation lights. The lower portion of the lights were blacked out. The only way you could see the lights was from above the helicopter or at the same level. This gave us a lot of protection from ground fire. Even though the enemy could hear the helicopter, in the pitch dark it was difficult to determine where it was.

"We'll fire one flare and give you covering fire," said the

infantryman. "You'll have to get the ammo to us though because we'll be out after we cover you." The flare erupted 200 yards away to our right. We spotted the small clearing and Stickney nosed the landing zone over and accelerated toward the opening. As we approached the clearing we began taking fire from the thick foliage. A mass of tracers began raking the jungle. Our soldiers were pouring on the covering fire. Stickney was making a vertical descent, the rotor blades barely clearing the trees. "Get on the controls with me," he said. "If I get hit you'll be on the controls already. Perez, you throw the ammo out and the gunner keep firing," he told the crewchief. Just as Perez began to throw the ammunition out, the flared flickered and went out. Stickney immediately flipped the landing light on. We could not afford to drift in any direction or the blades would be in the trees.

In a matter of seconds, the crewchief had the supplies off and screamed "go!" into the intercom. Stickney pulled power and we shot straight up. After clearing the trees, he turned the landing lights off and we headed back to Landing Zone Oasis. Amazingly, we had taken only one hit through the right landing skid.

On August 25th 1966, Operation "Paul Revere II" came to a close. By body count, the enemy had lost over 850 men.

7

Phan Thiet

Thinking we would get a few days rest back at An Khe, we were surprised to learn that we would be going directly to Phan Thiet, a coastal town about 150 miles southeast. The 2nd Battalion of the 7th Cavalry was already enroute, having left Pleiku on Air Force C-130 Hercules aircraft.

"Charlie" Company's helicopters topped off with fuel at Pleiku and departed for Phan Thiet. I was assigned to fly with Captain Ehnman. We were told to stop by An Khe, our home base, and pick up mail, aircraft parts and personal belongings that the air crewmen needed. Departing An Khe we climbed to nine thousand feet and had a relaxing flight to Phan Thiet. Looking down on the rice paddies around Tuy Hoa, it was hard to believe the death and destruction taking place in such a beautiful countryside.

We landed at the airfield just south of the town. It had been built by the French during the French Indo-China War. There was also a South Vietnamese training camp adjacent to the airstrip. C. Company was setting up camp just south of the airstrip. The grass was waist high over the whole area. My immediate concern was the probability of the place being the home of poisonous snakes. I would feel more comfortable facing a dozen Viet Cong in hand-to-hand combat rather than one snake, of any kind.

Two days after arriving at Phan Thiet, my fear of snakes being in the area was confirmed. The operations sergeant was in his tent and had just opened his laundry bag to put some dirty clothes in. As he started to push the clothes into the bag, a cobra suddenly thrust its head out of the opening. The sergeant let out a bloodcurdling scream and ran out the back of the tent. As he ran through the opening, he hit a tent rope, catching him in the neck and knocking him to the ground. Everyone in the area had heard him scream and went running over to where the sergeant was lying and gasping for air. After getting his breath, he was able to tell us about the cobra in his laundry bag. Sergeant Lynn put his M16 on full automatic and stepped cautiously inside the tent. Looking around he saw the laundry bag with a bulge in the side. He then proceeded to fire a whole clip of ammo into the bag. Unknown to us, the snake had crawled out of the bag and slipped out of the front of the tent.

Sergeant Lynn reached out with the barrel of his rifle and probed the bag. Warily, he picked the bag up and began to shake the clothes out. Emptying the bag and not finding the snake, the sergeant began holding up the ventilated clothing, some of them still smoldering from the tracer rounds that had gone into them.

The operations sergeant, having recovered from his bout

with the tent rope, saw his bullet-riddled clothes and went into a cussing fit. Sergeant Lynn seeing his opportunity, went the route of the cobra and slipped out the front of the tent, running for the safety of his own tent.

This was a relaxing bit of humor and quite a change after the stress and action we had just come from. I had survived my first month in Vietnam. I had eleven more to go.

8

Paddies of Death

The mission of the 2nd Battalion, 7th Cavalry, upon arrival at Phan Thiet, was to support the Vietnamese Revolutionary Development Program. They were to conduct search and destroy operations and provide protection for the Vietnamese while they harvested their rice crops.

The combat assaults commenced immediately and the task of finding and destroying the enemy was underway.

The terrain around the Phan Thiet area of operations was totally different from what our company had been used to. The coastal area of the South China Sea was mostly flat and consisted of thousands of acres of rice paddies, dotted with numerous villages and hamlets.

Through intelligence and the interrogation of captured Viet Cong, it was learned that the VC were coming into the villages after dark to obtain supplies for their units and to terrorize the local inhabitants. Some villages were also known to openly support the Viet Cong. In most cases the VC would remain in the villages overnight, leaving just prior to sunup.

We would usually have our pilots' briefing the night before the assault. We were told the village, coordinates, radio frequencies and any other pertinent information. The normal MO, or method of operation, was to assault one end of the village. The infantry would then make a sweep down both sides of the hamlet and through the center, checking each hooch or house as they went. Viet Cong suspects would be detained and transported back to base camp for interrogation. The problem with his MO was that some of the Viet Cong would slip out of the village while the infantry sweep was in progress. The VC would hold until the helicopters were out of sight and then make their break. After this flaw was discovered, it was decided to have one helicopter, with a squad of infantry, patrol the village during the sweep. This unique system soon became known as the "snatch" patrol.

The snatch patrol would fly in formation with the rest of the helicopters, but on final approach they would break out of formation and fly in the opposite direction. In the meantime the rest of the assault helicopters were dropping off the infantry troops. The slicks would then lift off and head back to base camp. Snatch patrol would turn toward the village and fly slowly above and in the same direction as the advancing skytroopers. When a Viet Cong would dart from the village, the snatch patrol helicopter would swoop down and intercept him. The infantrymen would jump off and capture the suspect. This was a very dangerous part of the operation. Often the VC would whirl around and start firing or hurl a grenade. In this case, the helicopter machinegun would open up with his M60 and kill the defiant VC.

In September of 1966, during a search and destroy operation, I was flying snatch patrol over a village just north of Phan Thiet. As we flew slowly above and slightly behind a squad of soldiers, a land mine suddenly erupted knocking several of the soldiers to the ground. At the same time an unknown number of enemy opened up with small arms fire. They were concealed in a tree line across a rice paddy from the village. The platoon leader requested that I land the squad soldiers behind the VC, on the opposite side of the tree line. We skirted the tree line and landed in a rice paddy approximately fifty yards from the tree line. Immediately we came under fire. One of the infantrymen took a hit in the upper leg as he was leaving the helicopter. The crewchief was laying down a withering fusillade with his M60 while the gunner tried to pull the wounded soldier back on board the helicopter. The other grunts were crawling through the water of the rice paddy toward the cover of a small dike. We lifted out of the rice paddy, the wounded soldier still partially outside of the helicopter. The platoon leader requested us to come back in and evacuate the men that had been wounded by the land mine. I had contacted the gunships escorting the assault helicopters back to base camp. They were enroute back to the firefight. Landing in a small clearing, with the soldiers still under fire, they began loading the other wounded men on board our helicopter. The booby trap had killed two of the soldiers and wounded three of them, two critically. The gunships arrived just as we were lifting off. They began to rake the thin strip of trees with rockets and machineguns. We were six minutes out of the field hospital located at Phan Thiet.

One of the soldiers had a severe head wound and was bleeding profusely. Another had his leg blown off between the knee and ankle. A piece of jagged white bone protruded from the severed leg. The third soldier wounded by the booby trap had a piece of shrapnel embedded in his arm. The helicopter crewchief worked feverishly trying to stem the bleeding of the soldier with the head wound. We landed at the Medevac pad where the medical personnel were waiting with the litters and emergency equipment. As they wheeled the wounded men toward the hospital tent, I saw them draw a sheet over one of them. For the soldier with the head wound, the war was over.

9

Incoming

It must have been around midnight. I could hear a dog barking off in the distance. The continuous yapping of the dog had jarred me out of semi-consciousness. I don't believe I had slept soundly since my arrival in Vietnam. The dog let out a sudden yelp as if it had been kicked or hit with a rock and then was silent. I lay in my sleeping bag surrounded by the ever-present mosquito netting, listening to the usual night sounds; the other pilots snoring softly, some mumbling in their sleep, the low steady hum of the generator at the operations tent and the sounds of the insects going about their nightly rituals.

To me, a round being fired from a mortar tube always sounded like a cork being pulled from a half empty cider jug. When I heard the "phoomp," I knew the usual three or four times a week mortar attack had begun. I pulled the mosquito netting loose and rolled out of the cot, dropping down into the little pit that Owens and I had dug weeks earlier. We had dug a bunker outside of the tent, sandbagged it up, covered it with P.S.P. and sandbags, but very seldom could we get to it during a mortar attack. We had decided to crowd our living space back some and dig the pit in the space between us. We had sandbagged the sides to keep the walls from crumbling in and installed a wooden floor using boards from ammunition boxes the artillery men had given us.

Just as I hit the floor, the first round detonated somewhere near the runway. "Incoming," I screamed. The pilots that hadn't awakened on the impact of the first mortar, were now scurrying for their bunkers.

Up to now we had only been attacked with mortar fire. Suddenly, automatic weapons began to open up on the south edge of our camp. A ground attack was underway. Sergeant Lynn ran down to our tent to tell the standby pilots to launch their helicopter immediately. The standby helicopter and crew were assigned every evening and were to fly high over the camp, dropping flares in the event of an attack. The gunships were to launch also. As one of the gunship pilots ran from his tent, a mortar round hit the corner of the entrance just as the pilot reached the opening. The blast tore the front of the tent to shreds and hurled the pilot to the ground. He lay silently in a pool of blood, critically wounded.

The flare ship leveled off at fifteen hundred feet above the camp and began dropping the flares. As the first flare bathed the camp in eerie light, one of the gunships began a run on the ground attack.

Several Viet Cong had reached the concertina wire and were trying to breach the perimeter. The gunship rolled out parallel and directly over the wire barrier. At full bore and low level, the gunship fired the 17-pound rockets in pairs.

The helicopter covered the length of the south perimeter in seconds. He pulled up in a steep left climb as the second gunship commenced the run in the same manner. The door gunners were covering the flanks of the helicopters and were firing on amy movement outside the perimeter.

The gunships broke off the attack and went into an orbiting pattern just above the flare ship. The mortars had ceased firing and the small arms fire had dwindled off to just a few random shots.

As I raised up to take another look, I heard a shot and then the metallic tearing of a bullet as it hit a GI water can a few feet to my left. The bullet continued around and around inside the can; sounding like a cowbell gone crazy.

As a fresh flare burst into life, I could see several of the enemy bodies draped over the barbed wire. The bodies and wire bobbed up and down as if floating on an invisible sea.

The following morning at zero four hundred, everyone was up and preparing for the first assault of the day. Two assault helicopters and the CO's jeep had sustained light shrapnel damage from the attack.

The crewchiefs and gunners had stayed up the remainder of the night, checking out the aircraft thoroughly, to insure their flight readiness for the following day.

This was an added burden for the helicopter air crewmen. They not only had to keep the aircraft in top mechanical condition, but they were required to fly all day on the air assaults and resupply missions. In addition, they also had to stand perimeter guard duty at night, for our sector of the base camp. The pilots stood officer-of-the-day duty, but only about once every two weeks.

After making three different air assaults into three villages, we were directed to return to base and were put on a standby basis with the Infantry Ready Reaction Force.

We would usually take this opportunity to have our

breakfast. Several of the pilots were sitting at the table in the mess tent, discussing the mortar and ground attack of the night before. The pilot that had been wounded from the mortar, had been air evacuated to Vung Tau and would probably go on to a hospital in Japan.

"Has anyone noticed that every time we get mortared, none of those slopes show up to work on the runway?" asked "Surf" Owen.

The Army had hired some of the local people from Phan Thiet to do various jobs around the camp and airfield. They had a crew working on the runway at nights, filling potholes and smoothing out the rough spots.

"I hadn't thought too much about it before, but I believe you are right, Surf," added Doug Clyde.

"Yeah, come to think of it, those fishing boats are always way off shore on the nights we get hit, also," I said.

Our base camp was situated on a bluff overlooking the South China Sea. Normally the fishing fleet lay fairly close to shore, but on certain nights, you could see the lights of the boats shining several miles out.

"You guys might have something," said Captain May. "I'll go and talk to the CO and let him know about this."

About fifteen minutes later, Major Blanton, who had recently assumed command from Major Williams, drove over to the 2nd of the 7th's Battalion Headquarters, located on the east end of the airfield.

An hour later, Major Blanton called a pilots meeting. "I talked to the Battalion CO and he agrees, there might be something to this matter. That would explain why they always walk those mortar rounds up through the helicopters and the runway," he added. "They are going to set up a watch on the runway crew and see if they can nab the VC bastard."

For the next several nights, the locals worked on the

runway under the big flood lights, as they normally did. The fishing boats were tucked in close to shore. Everything was routine.

The third night, just as it was getting dark, the fishing boats began ambling out to sea. The runway work crew would usually be setting up the flood lights about this time, but they hadn't shown up for work.

"OK, we think they are going to hit us tonight," said Major Blanton. "I want the flare ship crew standing by the aircraft and ready to launch. I also want the gunships ready to go. I want one ship cranked and running at flight idle. Shut down after fifteen minutes and let the other gunship run at idle for fifteen minutes. Hover down and refuel whenever necessary," he continued. "We have doubled the perimeter guards and the Ready Reaction Force is also on standby."

At twenty-three hundred hours, the first mortar round slammed into the runway about midfield. The idling gunship came up to full power and lifted off. He climbed out in a tight turn, staying over the camp. The flare ship and the other gunship started up and launched.

"I just saw a flash of fire on the west edge of the cemetery," said Captain Parker, the aircraft commander of one of the gunships.

"Roger, we're headed over that way," said Warrant Officer Erkhart, the flare ship pilot. The UHF radio was on in the operations tent and I could hear most of the chatter between the pilots of the airborne helicopters.

The first flare popped, showering the cemetery northwest of our camp with a brilliant light. I could see the gunships darting about searching the cemetery. "All right, I've got the little bastards spotted," the gunship pilot said suddenly. "Keep those flares popping. I'm going hot and starting a run on them now." The gunship made a diving left turn and lined up on the enemy mortar crew. The 2.75-inch rockets made a frightening noise as they wooshed away from the rocket pods. They burst in rapid succession as the gunship pulled up. The second gunship rolled in on the target with his machineguns spewing tracers into the same area.

"I saw three of them flatten out," said Captain Prestipino, AC of the second gunship. "I think you stitched them real good," he said to Parker. "OK, we're going to swing around the perimeter and see if anything else is happening on the south side." The anticipated ground attack never materialized.

The following morning, an infantry patrol walked out to where the enemy mortar crew were lying. The mortar tube was damaged and laying among the dead VC. One of the gunship's rockets had hit a tombstone, shattering it and sending a jagged chuck of stone into the back of one of the fleeing Cong.

One of the dead VC was identified as one of the runway work crew. He had the job operating the roller. It was determined that he had been marking off the distance and range for the mortar attacks. It was to be more than a week before we would have another mortar attack.

10

His Brother's Keeper

"**L**urkey" Dave Durling had the day off. Like the rest of us, he welcomed the break from combat flying and the chance to relax. Lt. Durling had been waiting for a chance to visit an old buddy, based close by.

He arrived at his friend's camp only to find him about to take off. His friend was a light observation helicopter pilot and was scheduled for a routine patrol flight about twenty miles north of Phan Thiet.

"Why don't you ride along with me?" asked the friend. "It will only be about an hour flight and then we can come back and drink some cold beers while we B.S.".

Durling agreed. The crewchief checked him out on the operation of the M60 machinegun mounted on the small helicopter.

The two friends lifted off. Flying a few hundred feet above the ground, the OH-13 swept back and forth searching for any enemy activity. Suddenly, bullets ripped into the helicopter, shattering the Plexiglas bubble and the instrument panel. The helicopter yawed back and forth and went into a spinning dive with the pilot slumped over the cyclic control stick. The pilot had taken several hits in his legs and left shoulder. Durling was unscathed. He struggled with his friend's unconscious body, trying to pull him from the controls. Leaning across his wounded buddy, Durling grabbed the controls and leveled the aircraft just prior to impact. The helicopter hit hard, flexing the main rotor blades down into the tailboom and sending shattered pieces of blade in all directions. Durling managed to transmit a Mayday and his approximate location. He then shut off all the switches, unbuckled his friend's seat belt and pulled him from the wreckage. Fearing fire and an explosion from the smoldering helicopter, Durling dragged the wounded pilot several yards into the brush and then dashed back to the wreck to grab the M60 machinegun.

Just as he reached the downed helicopter, several Viet Cong opened up on him with small arms fire. Durling ripped the machinegun from its Bungee cord mountings, grabbed the ammo can and raced back to his wounded companion.

The Viet Cong moved cautiously toward the downed pilots. Durling set the machinegun up on a small mound of dirt. The crashed helicopter was between him and the enemy, but the VC had spread out and were attempting to outflank him and the wounded pilot. He slipped the safety off the .30-caliber machinegun and raked the heavy brush with several bursts of fire. The firing stopped the Cong's advance. They had flattened out and could only fire in the general direction of the airmen. Durling now attempted to attend to his friend's wounds. He bandaged and applied pressure to the bleeding wounds.

Every few minutes he would crawl back to the machinegun and spray the brush with bullets. He had been so busy in the first few minutes of the furious action that he had not considered the futile situation he was in. He now began to evaluate the options. If he didn't get medical attention for his friend soon, he would probably die from his wounds. If he surrendered, there was no guarantee that the Viet Cong would let them live, either.

It was a well-known fact that the VC had a distinct hatred for the American helicopter crews. In some cases, it was reported that some American pilots were hung by their arms and skinned alive.

Durling decided to fight and hoped that his Mayday distress call had been heard. He figured that the Viet Cong patrol was probably no more than six or seven men. However, there might be more enemy soldiers on the way. Fighting would buy a little time. If it looked as if they would be overrun, he would give up in order to save his friend, hoping the VC would take them prisoners and not kill them.

Another problem facing him, was that he was running low on ammunition for the machinegun.

Durling heard movement off to his right. The VC were crawling through the brush trying to encircle the two pilots. He swung the gun around and swept the heavy undergrowth with bullets, firing just above ground level. An enemy soldier screamed in pain. He stopped firing. As the roar of the machinegun subsided, he could barely hear the unmistakable rotor beat of the approaching Hueys. He prayed that the helicopter crews would be able to spot the downed OH-13. He now wished that the little observation helicopter had caught fire as the smoke would have guided the rescue helicopters right to them.

The Viet Cong recognized the dreaded sound of the helicopters also. They began to withdraw through the brush, dragging their wounded comrade with them.

Durling saw the helicopters about a quarter mile south of his position. "They are going to fly right by us," he said aloud. Suddenly the lead helicopter made a sharp left turn and headed straight for the wrecked helicopter. The first Huey came to a hover directly above the OH-13. The second helicopter set up an orbit around the downed ship and airmen. Durling waved frantically at the hovering helicopter. The crewchief spotted him and waved back in recognition.

The circling gunship spotted the retreating Viet Cong and went on the attack. The helicopter over the downed OH-13 hovered over to Durling and the wounded pilot.

Unable to land because of the high brush, the helicopter hovered above the downed pilots while the crewchief dropped the five feet from the skid of the helicopter into the brush. Durling and the crewchief boosted the unconscious pilot up to the open door of the Huey. The gunner pulled him into the helicopter, laying him gently on the floor. Durling was next. He crawled onto the skid and then into the ship. The crewchief handed the machinegun to the gunner and swung easily onto the skid and into the helicopter.

The helicopters pulled out and returned to Phan Thiet. Within an hour, a crew had rigged the downed helicopter and slung it back to Phan Thiet.

After seeing his friend safely off to the field hospital, Durling returned to our company area. Asked about how he had enjoyed his day off, he shrugged his shoulders, crawled into his bunk and went to sleep.

11

Battle of Phan Thiet

Daybreak over the South China Sea is one of the few good memories of the Vietnam War I'm not likely to forget. The multitude of colors, just prior to sunrise, is an unforgettable sight. The different shades of pink blended with various purples, glistening off a perfectly calm sea, gave me a brief glimpse of the peaceful beauty that can touch a land such as this; a country locked in war and violent death.

The twenty-fifth of October 1966 was such a day. After watching the new day begin, I was brought back to reality and the business of war as the high-pitched whine of the helicopter's jet engines broke the morning stillness.

There was no reason to believe that this day would be any different than the previous one. My company had been air assaulting various areas and villages, carrying skytroopers of the 7th Cavalry.

After completing several assaults, we returned to Phan Thiet and were put on a standby status.

Around 1400 hours, a light observation OH-13 helicopter spotted an estimated company of Viet Cong.

The helicopter pilot radioed the enemy's position and then began an attack with the door gunner firing his M60 machinegun. Two Aerial Rocket Artillery helicopters on patrol in another sector were diverted to the enemy's location. The enemy force, taken completely by surprise, began digging in where they stood. The enemy had been caught in the open while crossing a series of fields and rice paddies.

The Infantry Ready Reaction Force had been lounging around the helicopters. They were loaded and airborne within five minutes upon receiving the order to attack.

In fifteen minutes, we had covered the twenty-five air miles and were setting up for the assault. It was decided to go in right on top of the enemy. The Battalion Commander, Lt. Colonel Vaughn, flying in the Command and Control helicopter, advised the pilots of the assault helicopters to have the infantrymen on board their aircraft fix bayonets.

I turned around and told the squad leader, sitting behind me, what was going on. As the grunts attached the bayonets to their rifles, they began whooping and shouting, working themselves into a frenzy.

I imagined this had taken place a thousand times before, prior to soldiers being only minutes away from a battle.

For a moment, I wondered if Custer's troopers had reacted like this just prior to Little Big Horn. Ninety years previous, soldiers of the 7th Cavalry, the very unit I was now hauling into battle, had died in a desperate struggle with overwhelming odds. How would this fight turn out? My heart raced wildly.

The soldiers on my ship reminded me of high school kids getting hyped-up just before a football game. Undoubtedly, most of them were probably only a year or two out of high school.

My fellow air crewman and I joined in on the increasing crescendo of excitement, now at a feverish pitch.

This type of behavior, I reasoned later, had to be the controlling factor that kept soldiers from the breaking point, whenever they faced the unknown outcome of imminent danger.

The eight assault helicopters carrying the two platoons of C Company, 2nd of the 7th Cavalry, started into the landing zone in staggered trail formation. It was decided that all eight ships would go in simultaneously since the landing zone was large enough to accommodate them. My helicopter, White Two, would be the sixth helicopter in the formation, thus putting me somewhere near the middle of the LZ and the Bad Guys.

On short final, all hell broke loose. The gunships escorting the troop carrying slicks, began their attack down each side of the landing zone. The gunship on the right of the formation had a grenade launcher mounted on the nose. The pilot was yawing the helicopter back and forth, spewing grenades throughout the LZ. By working the directional control pedals back and forth, as in the manner of a child's pedal car, the gunship pilots had found a technique to maximize the gunship's deadly role in combat.

The door gunners on the slicks began firing their machine-guns. The enemy was firing back from their shallow foxholes. Some of the Viet Cong broke from the holes and were running toward a tree line a hundred yards away. I never saw any of them make it.

A few feet from the ground, the cavalrymen began jumping from the helicopters, firing while in mid-air. As was their habit, many of the soldiers were already outside the helicopters. The last hundred yards, they would step out on the skids holding on with one hand and firing their weapons with the other.

I suddenly realized I hadn't lowered the visor on my helmet. Remembering the pilots who had been blinded a few months earlier by shattered Plexiglas, I made a quick attempt to lower the visor, but was unable to do it. I had to re-grab the collective control with my left hand just prior to touchdown.

As we paused momentarily to discharge the remainder of the grunts, an enemy soldier abruptly popped up from a hole about five yards from my left front. He must have thought that we had singled him out to land on. The communist soldier went on the attack.

With my hands still on the controls and holding the helicopter light on the skids, I was completely helpless as the enemy soldier raised his rifle.

I looked into his eyes. The fear on his face was a reflection of what he must have seen on mine. I tried to shrink down a little farther behind the armored plating on my left side, but still felt exposed to the world.

I don't know if the VC ever got a shot off or not. The next thing I saw was him going down with a bayonet running through his neck. He was still staring at me, but now with a look of disbelief on his face.

The last helicopter in the flight radioed that the flight was up. Meaning all the infantrymen were clear of the ships and we were free to lift off.

Just as I lifted the helicopter off the ground, the soldier who had bayoneted the Viet Cong, placed his boot on the dead soldier's head and pulled the bayonet free.

He glanced at me briefly as I nosed the helicopter over to depart the landing zone.

Unable to take my hands from the controls to wave, I nodded my head several times in gratitude. The soldier was the squad leader I had spoken to only minutes earlier. I felt that if it wasn't for him, my aviation career would probably had ended abruptly. He waved his M16 and was gone.

We lifted out of the landing zone and returned to Phan Thiet where we were again on standby in the event the platoons of Charlie Company needed reinforcements.

The Battle of Phan Thiet was over in three hours. We went back into the landing zone to extract the cavalrymen. The enemy had lost fifty-two soldiers, most of them killed in the first few minutes of the fierce hand-to-hand combat.

During the process of mopping up, one American soldier was killed by a concealed sniper.

I prayed that it wasn't the squad leader who had saved my life. I never found out.

12

The Flying Beer Truck

Nearly two weeks had passed since our company had received an allotment of beer. We had dug a pit, sand bagged up the sides and put a roof over the whole thing. This served as a cooler for our beer whenever we did get a shipment.

We would buy ice in Phan Thiet to put in the cooler, but we were reluctant to buy the local beer because of the experiences we had in Pleiku, a few months earlier. The Viet Cong had put ground glass and poison in a lot of the soft drinks and beer. Several American soldiers had died and others had become extremely sick or injured.

Major Blanton told my crew and me to fly down to Vung Tau and get a load of beer. If we couldn't get it there, we were to go to Saigon. In so many words, we were not to come back without the refreshments.

We flew along the coastline enroute to Vaug Tau. An hour later, we were on the ground at the airfield. The parking ramp was crowded with row after row of new helicopters that had arrived by ship from the United States. I had been down here before, a couple of times, to pick up replacement helicopters for our company.

I walked over to the Operations Office. The sergeant on duty loaned us a Jeep and we drove over to the Base Commissary. Asking to see the officer in charge, I was directed to an office in the back of the store. I opened the door and walked in, a staff sergeant was sitting at a desk piled high with papers and invoices.

"Morning, Sarg. I'm wondering, what would be the chances of getting a few cases of beer?" I asked.

Before the sergeant had a chance to answer, a pimply faced second lieutenant emerged from a back office. "I'm in charge here and anything that leaves this store has to be cleared through me," he barked. "Besides, what makes you think we should sell you people anything?" he continued. "You 1st Cavalry people think that all you have to do is walk into a place and everyone should cater to your every whim," he rattled on, eyeing the Cavalry patch on my grubby jungle shirt.

"Lieutenant, all we want is a few cases of beer. We're based in Phan Thiet and this is the closest place to get some," I said.

"Well, I'm not furnishing anything for you people. Go to An Khe and get it. You Cavalry people are all alike. You think that you're the only ones fighting this war," he said.

I looked at the sergeant. He shook his head in disgust and embarrassment. "Lieutenant, I didn't come all the way down here to receive a lecture from you. Furthermore, I can't understand why they would put an idiot in charge of a commissary in the first place. As far as your beer is concerned, take it and shove it, you asshole,'' I shouted angrily.

"I'll have you court martialed,'' he shot back.

"Yeah, and I'm going to smack you in your smartass mouth if you say anything more,'' I said, moving toward him. He headed for his office. I turned and walked out of the office, slamming the door as I left.

As I was getting into the Jeep, where the other three crew members were waiting, the sergeant came hurrying out of the commissary. "Sir, wait a minute,'' he said. "I'm sorry the lieutenant acted that way. He's a little frustrated because he's stuck with that job,'' he went on.

"You don't have to apologize for him, Sarg, it isn't your fault,'' I said.

"Well, there wouldn't have been any problem if he hadn't overheard us. I'm going to go ahead and get the beer for you. How many cases do you want?'' he asked.

"We'll take as many as we can get. I'd like to get enough for our company and the gunship platoon,'' I answered.

"OK, it'll take about an hour to load it. Let me have the tail number of your ship and I'll have it delivered to the airfield.''

"It's six-two-three and we're parked on the west side ramp,'' I replied. "Do you want us to help load it?''

"Na, I've got people laying on their butts that are getting paid to do it.''

We ran several more errands and then headed for the air field. After a twenty minute wait, a deuce and a half truck pulled up to our helicopter. The sergeant and the driver got out. Two more soldiers jumped down from the back of the truck, dropped the tailgate and began unloading the beer. The truck was about three-quarters full of several different brands of beer.

"I don't believe we'll get all that beer on the ship, Sarg," I said.

"That's all right, you guys take what you want and I'll unload the rest over at air operations," he answered.

The crewchief and gunner were busy stacking the cases of beer in the helicopter. The seat where they normally sat were folded up and the space filled to capacity with cases of beer.

"Sir, I think we have about all the weight we can handle," said Johnson, the crewchief.

"Keep stacking it on. Leave yourselves enough room to ride behind the pilots' seats," I replied. Finally, we were unable to squeeze another case of beer on board.

"We'll never get off the ground," the co-pilot stated. I was beginning to have doubts myself. "What do we owe you for all of this?" I asked the sergeant.

"Nothing, Sir, we're glad to get it for you," he answered.

"I don't want to see you get in trouble over this, Sergeant. You'll have to account for it somehow."

"No problem. I could give you a thousand cases and they would never miss it. We've got tons of stuff around here that we don't even know about yet."

"Well, here's a hundred bucks anyway. We expected to pay more than that," I said, handing him the military script.

"Thank you, Sir. Any time you need something, come and see me first. Forget the lieutenant," he said, getting into the truck.

We got into the helicopter and I started the turbine engine. I rolled the throttle up to operating r.p.m. "We'd better see if she'll lift off before we call the tower," I said over the intercom. I started pulling up on the collective control. The collective changes the pitch of the rotor blades to make the helicopter ascend or descend. I had maximum pitch pulled in but the helicopter still hadn't broken ground.

The exhaust gas temperature on the turbine engine was riding right at red line. "We're going to have to throw some of the beer off, Sir," said Johnson, peering at the gauges over my shoulder.

"Negative, none of the beer goes off," I replied. "I've got an idea. I think we can make a running takeoff."

"How in the hell are you going to get it to the runway?" asked the co-pilot, "If you try to slide the helicopter on this steel planking, they'll hang up and dump us." He was worried about the skids catching on the perforations in the steel planking. The planking was used for taxi and parking areas. The co-pilot had a legitimate argument, but I ignored the statement.

"Johnson, you and Brown jump out and beat it over the runway and wait for us. The loss of three hundred and fifty pounds should let us get off the ground enough to get us to the runway," I said. Johnson and Brown jumped out and headed out at a trot.

"Vung Tau Tower, Army Helicopter Six-Two-Three," I called over the UHF radio. "Six-Two-Three, Vung Tau," came the reply.

"Vung Tau-Six-Two-Three, I would like to hover out to the runway and make a practice running takeoff," I lied.

"Make a what?" came the response from the tower.

"A practice running takeoff."

"I've never heard of such a thing, but hover out and hold short of the runway. I've got a Mohawk on a half mile final," the tower operator stated.

"Roger," I replied.

Again I pulled in power. This time just as the engine temperature reached red line, the helicopter shuddered and reluctantly lifted off. As I nudged the ship forward it settled and plunked back onto the P.S.P. It immediately bounced back off the ground. We covered the whole hundred yards in this manner, bouncing like a pigged-out kangaroo. As we gained forward momentum, each bounce would carry us a little farther. Stopping just short of the runway, Johnson and Brown crawled back into the helicopter. The Mohawk touched down with little puffs of smoke rolling off the tires. The roar of the props being reversed, mingled with the noise of our rotor blades. It turned off the runway in front of us.

"Army helicopter Six-Two-Three clear for takeoff," said the controller. "Six-Two-Three, Roger," I replied.

Again I pulled in power but the helicopter would not lift off. "Damn," I said. "You guys jump back out until I get her moving," I told the now thoroughly disgusted crew. Johnson and Brown crawled back out.

They still had their helmets on and were plugged into the intercom system.

This time the helicopter started to slide a little but still hadn't broken ground. I nudged the stick forward, adding a little left pedal. The helicopter turned slowly and lined up with the runway. We began to pick up a little speed. Johnson and Brown were trotting along, one on each side of the helicopter. They had one hand on the partly opened doors and the other held their communication cords.

"Helicopter Six-Two-Three, what in the hell are you guys doing? Do you know you've got two people running alongside your ship?" came the astonished voice from the tower.

"Uh-Roger that tower, it's just part of our drill," I replied quickly. The helicopter lifted off about two inches above the runway. By this time, Johnson and Brown were in a dead run trying to keep up.

"OK, you guys, get on. I think we got 'er sacked," I shouted over the intercom.

Both crewmen jumped onto the skids simultaneously. The helicopter immediately plowed back onto the runway. The screeching and grinding noises of the skids against the asphalt runway was almost unbearable, but we continued to gain speed.

We had another problem confronting us now. We had started our takeoff on the last quarter of the runway and were now rapidly running out of room.

The screeching noise stopped abruptly as the helicopter vaulted off the runway to an altitude of about six inches.

"Yahoo," I screamed with glee. "I knew we could do it. I used to watch those guys on TV milk those B-17's off the runway on that show *12 O'clock High*."

The co-pilot was looking at me out of the corner of his eye. I'm sure he thought I should be bouncing off the walls of a rubber room somewhere, rather than bouncing a helicopter off a runway in Vietnam.

"Army Six-Two-Three, have you got the obstacle in sight, you're twelve o'clock position?" the controller asked, interrupting my thoughts. The other pilot and I began to scan the sky in front of us, looking for a radio tower or possibly another aircraft. "Negative," I replied. "No joy."

"Well, it's the barbed wire fence just off your nose. Do you guys want to call off your dinging around and get the hell out of my airspace?" said the voice from the tower. He was sounding very perplexed by now.

"Roger that tower. We're heading north. Request frequency change," I answered.

"Frequency change approved. Good day, Sir," he said than as an afterthought, "Good luck."

"Are we going to clear that wire," Johnson asked.

"Oh yeah, no sweat. The fence is only three or four feet high," I said.

"That could be real interesting," said the co-pilot. "We are currently only about two and a half feet off the ground," he added sarcastically.

"I'd better start throwing some of the beer off," said Johnson.

"Johnson, after going through all this, if you throw as much as one can of beer off, I'll have you boiled in Nhoc-mam," I shouted. Nhoc-mam is a rotten smelling sauce made from fish left out in the sun to ferment.

The co-pilot covered his eyes just before we reached the fence. I yanked the control stick back and then forward again. The helicopter porpoised up and over the wire, shuddering like a dog shaking off water. Clearing the wire, we were back to our two and a half feet of altitude still heading north. One by one, the co-pilot slowly peeled his fingers from his eyes. "You know," he said calmly, "if we get anywhere near the ground again, I'm going to get out of this son-of-a-bitch and walk back to base. I've given it a lot of thought. I could handle getting greased while flying in combat, or in a mortar attack, or just about any way there is to get killed in a war. But I can't bear to think of getting it while in a flying beer truck. I couldn't stand the thought of getting shipped home in a body bag smelling like a used bar rag from a gin mill on Tudo Street."

"I always wondered what it was like to fly a brick," I said, trying to be funny. "Now I know," I continued, ignoring the oratory the other pilot had just recited.

It took about ten miles but we managed to nurse the Huey up to five hundred feet. The best we could do on airspeed was seventy knots. "This calls for a celebration," I said. "Johnson, break open a case of that beer. I'm buying," I joked. Johnson and Brown had already dipped into the goodies and were working on their second beer.

"I should of had about a dozen of these before we took off," said Johnson as he handed two cans of Black Label forward. The beer was hot. I sipped on it slowly, trying to make myself enjoy the fruit of our labor.

In a little more than an hour, we arrived back in Phan Thiet. After burning off around five hundred pounds of fuel, the helicopter was still over its allowable gross weight. On short final the helicopter began descending rapidly. I made a run-on landing in the grassy area. The helicopter skidded to a halt. I was proud of the landing; I had spared our lives and had not damaged the ship.

The welcome back was like the pictures I'd seen of Lindbergh when he landed in Paris. The beer-thirsty soldiers mobbed the helicopter. Ignoring us, they began feverishly to unload the beer.

That evening after the beer had been iced down, the major presented us with blue ribbons; Pabst Blue Ribbons, that is. A better reward could not be found.

13

A Witness to Death

I was assigned Officer-of-the Day. It was the first time that I had to stand the duty since we had arrived in Phan Thiet. It was my responsibility to check the perimeter in our sector and to make sure all defensive gun emplacements were manned prior to sunset.

I was a little edgy. I had heard all of the stories about the O.D. being challenged at night, not remembering the password and getting waxed from the scene.

I decided that I would make my rounds while it was still light. I would get to know the men on duty that night and would also show them that I was really a nice guy and shouldn't be shot if I goofed up when making my rounds later that night.

I was driving the company commander's Jeep and began my rounds at the post on the northeast side of the airfield.

This particular emplacement overlooked the beach and the South China Sea. Up to this time, we had never been attacked from the ocean side. I chatted with the men briefly and helped them set up their weapons and gear for the night. Continuing around the south side, I repeated the scenario at each perimeter outpost.

As I drove up to the last bunker in my sector, another Jeep drove up and stopped short of the west end of the airstrip. A young soldier jumped out, grabbed his web gear and snatched his rifle, barrel first, from the backseat of the Jeep. As he pulled the rifle from the Jeep, I heard a shot. The soldier slumped to his knees. Still clutching the rifle, he fell backwards, sprawling into the red sand.

I ran to the fallen soldier. Several other soldiers had heard the shot and were running toward us.

The round had hit the soldier in the stomach. He lay on his back with blood and gurgling noises coming from his mouth. One of the soldiers was a medic and he began working desperately on the wounded man.

We were about fifty yards from the helicopter refueling point. A gunship had just landed and was taking on fuel. I ran over to the gunship, jumped up on the skid and told the pilot about the accident. I asked him to hover over to the wounded soldier so we could put him in the helicopter.

The field hospital was at the opposite end of the airfield, a little more than a mile. If we could get him to the hospital fast enough, he might have a chance.

By now the critically injured soldier had turned a sickening gray color. He was in deep shock.

We loaded him into the helicopter. The medic still worked feverishly trying to keep the soldier alive.

The gunship lifted off and flew at maximum speed to the hospital.

The whole ordeal lasted less than fifteen minutes, but it was too late. The soldier had received a mortal wound.

I found out from one of the other soldiers that the dead infantryman had been on search and destroy missions all day. It was his turn to stand perimeter guard duty that night. The soldier had been careless grabbing his rifle like he did, but he was tired and worn out.

It seemed like there never were enough people to do everything that had to be done. There never seemed to be enough time for proper rest. The soldier died doing his duty. It bothered me not knowing whether his death would be classified as a combat or non-combat death.

Several days had passed since the accident had taken place. I had seen many dead soldiers, but I couldn't stop thinking about this man's death. Maybe I felt responsible, somehow. I should have told him to slow up or something. I didn't know why I felt so much concern.

I saw the package first, as I walked into the tent. It was lying on my sweat-stained sleeping bag. One corner of the package was ripped out. Popcorn had rolled out through the hole and was scattered on the bunk. I knew the package was from Mom. She always packed the cookies, cigars and other things she sent in popcorn. This helped to keep the goodies fresh and kept most of the things from getting crushed. It also did one other thing. I always wondered why my ''Care'' packages had holes in them. I finally figured out that wherever the packages were lying after they arrived in Vietnam, it must be in a place where there were rats. The rats would chew into the package and then eat on the popcorn.

A letter was lying on the package, tucked under the twine that bound the package. I recognized Mom's writing. I pushed the package aside and sat down. A cold chill came over me as I picked up the letter. I didn't want to open it. I tore the envelope down the left side, a habit of mine. I never like to open a letter in a manner to mutilate the stamp.

Dear Buz,

. This is one of those letters I don't like to write.

Granma died today.

I couldn't read any further. I repeated it over and over in my mind. Granma died today. Granma died today.

I sat on the edge of the ammo box bed, slumped over, staring at the letter.

"Good popcorn, Sisk," I heard someone say. I looked up. Owen was standing there shoving popcorn into his mouth.

"Don't eat that shit, man," I said with tears streaming down my face. Owen stopped, frozen with a handful of popcorn in his mouth. "Rats been eating on it," I sobbed.

"What's wrong? What's wrong?" Owen asked, dropping the popcorn. "A death in my family," I said quietly.

"I'm real sorry," Owen said softly. He walked over and lay down on his bunk.

I read the rest of the letter. Mom told me how they had contacted the Red Cross to see if I could be brought home for Gram's funeral. They said because she wasn't immediate family, that I would not be authorized to go home.

The date on the letterhead showed that the letter had been written on the same day that I had Officer-of-the-Day. Gram was on her deathbed at the time I was helping to save, or trying to save the life of the gut-shot trooper.

I pulled a beer out of my private cooler. I had buried a parts can in the center of my floor. It was big enough to hold about twelve beers and some ice to keep it cold.

I sipped on the beer silently, toasting Granma and wishing her all the best. May she rest in peace.

"Hey, Sisk, what 'n the hell you doing drinking beer?

You've more flying to do,'' someone said as he passed through the tent.

"Stick it in your ear," Surf Owen shouted. "I'm doing his flying the rest of the day."

"You don't have to do that, Surf. I'll be OK," I said.

"Ah, hell with it. I'll fill in for you. All we got is ash and trash runs anyway. If we go out on some assaults, you'll probably have to go. I think they'll need all the ships and all the pilots. We've got a couple of guys out on R&R, so we would be shorthanded."

Nothing unusual happened the rest of the day. I continued drinking the beers. I awoke the next morning feeling slightly hung over but nevertheless anxious for the day's assaults and flying to begin.

14

The Flying Wounded

F lying the "Charlie-Charlie" helicopter was usually a
good assignment. Charlie-Charlie was short for Command and Control.

In this modern day combat, the Battlefield Commander
would fly over the area of operations, controlling the battle
and strategy from his airborne command post. From this
lofty position, he had direct and constant communications
with the units on the ground, the artillery and air support.

Warrant Officer Doug Clyde was assigned the task of
flying the Charlie-Charlie ship. Clyde and his crew hovered
the helicopter over to Battalion Headquarters to have the
communications equipment installed.

The Battalion CO, the Executive Officer and the Artillery
Officer arrived. The mission was to be a recon over a
suspected enemy location. If the recon indicated that the

enemy was indeed active in the area, then a helicopter air assault would be planned.

The aircraft departed to the north-northwest and was soon over the area.

"I need to be lower," said the Battalion CO. "We've had reports on aircraft being fired on and hit in this area," responded Clyde. "One aircraft was hit with fifty caliber stuff," he added.

"I don't give a damn. I need to get lower to get a good look."

Clyde began a circling descent. Flashes of gunfire would, at times, look similar to dew sparkling off a green lawn. Even in daytime, weapons fired from dark foliage or a tree line would emit a visible muzzle flash.

"We're taking fire," the crewchief shouted over the intercom. Clyde pulled back on the cyclid stick. As the helicopter nosed up into an immediate climb, bullets slammed into its belly. Clyde felt a searing pain in both legs. At the very instant he was hit, he heard a loud scream. He wasn't too sure if he was the one who had screamed or not. He scanned the instrument panel, checking gauges. Everything appeared to be all right.

"Take the controls," he told the co-pilot. "I'm hit and my legs are going numb. Head back to the airfield. Crewchief, give me a report on everyone back there," Clyde said, looking back over his seat.

The colonel was stretched out on the floor of the Huey, lying face down.

"The colonel is the only one hit back here," said the crewchief. "It looks like he got it in the ass, Sir."

Getting shot in the rear end or the privates is probably the worst fear that people flying in combat can have. The pilots' seats on the Huey have armored plating underneath and around the back and sides. The rest of the aircraft is vulnerable. A bullet had ripped through the sheet metal of the helicopter directly under Clyde's seat. It then smashed into the armored plating and ricocheted between his legs, exiting through the Plexiglas chin bubble. Pieces of the floor decking and chips from the armored plating peppered the backside of Clyde's lower legs like a shotgun blast. Blood ran down his legs, over his boots and onto the floor.

The colonel was lying quite still. He was moaning a little as the wound was painful.

Clyde called our company operations on the UHF radio and notified them that they were inbound to the field hospital with two wounded on board. The operations officer acknowledged the radio message. He then called the hospital by telephone. The medical personnel would be standing by at the heliport.

The helicopter touched down and the co-pilot shut down the engine.

The colonel was placed on a stretcher facedown. A doctor began treating the wound trying to stem the bleeding.

Clyde was helped out of the cockpit, and was carried to the emergency tent. They worked on him several hours extracting the little chunks of metal splinters from his legs. He was released from the hospital the next day; given two days off and then placed back on active flying status.

The colonel had been very lucky also. A bullet had come up through the flooring, through the canvas jump seat the colonel was sitting on and then through his billfold into his buttock. The bullet had been slowed considerably by the billfold. After penetrating the billfold, the bullet had fishhooked back around into the colonel's butt, causing quite a bit of bleeding but very little damage otherwise.

Christmas was not going to be good for any of us. Spending it in Vietnam and away from families would be disheartening, to say the least.

For Warrant Officer Robert Curtis it would be a day for flirtation with death.

There was to be an unofficial truce Christmas Day. We were on a "stand down." In other words, we were not to do any fighting or air assaults during this twenty-four-hour period.

In the past, however, the enemy had used these stand downs to move people and equipment into attack position. The concensus was that this holiday would be no different.

The regular helicopter patrols would continue, regardless of the stand down. The only difference was that we were not to engage the enemy unless we were fired on first.

Early Christmas morning, 1966. Curtis lifted off Phan Thiet, the "Dawn Patrol," as we called it. He departed to the north to begin the recon. This would be the same sector where we had trouble in before. It was also close to where Clyde had been hit a few weeks earlier.

Curtis spotted a column of men working their way, snake-like, through heavy brush and undergrowth. Knowing that no American or Allied troops were supposed to be on patrol, he orbited the people on the ground. The soldiers had scattered and were hiding in the brush.

This pretty well convinced him that it was an enemy unit on the move. As he keyed his microphone to report his find, the instrument panel in front of him exploded into chunks of metal and fiberglass. The bullets had ripped into the nose of the helicopter, into the instrument panel, with some of them exiting through the roof of the helicopter into the rotor system. One bullet had knocked the altitude indicator completely out of its mounting. Either a bullet or a piece of flying jagged metal then smashed into Curtis' jaw, knocking him unconscious. The helicopter turned violently, on the verge of being out of control. The co-pilot who had just recently checked into our unit, grabbed the controls and leveled the aircraft.

The co-pilot turned the aircraft south and radioed a Mayday. Not knowing the damage sustained by the helicopter, he wanted some help on the way, in case they went down.

A Huey gunship was launched from Phan Thiet. Curtis had regained semi-consciousness. The crewchief and gunner had pulled the quick release pins on his set. This allowed them to tilt the set back where they could unfasten his seat belt and shoulder harness. They slid him slowly out of the seat and stretched him out on the floor of the helicopter.

In the meantime, the gunship had spotted the damaged slick. They made radio contact with the co-pilot and made a turn, rolling out even with Curtis' ship.

The two helicopters returned to Phan Thiet with no further problems. The co-pilot landed the helicopter at the medical pad and Curtis was wheeled to the emergency tent.

The bullet had traveled through the fleshy part of his chin just below the bone. Again luck had been with one of the pilots. Curtis was off two days and then put back on flying status. He flew a week with his face still in bandages.

Short of being killed, I wondered how bad a pilot had to be wounded before he no longer had to fly in combat. I also hoped I'd never find out.

Warrant Officer candidates Robert Sisk and Brian Pray. Flight school—Fort Wolters, Texas. December, 1965. (All photos courtesy of Robert W. Sisk)

Aerial Rocket Attack Helicopter, commonly called a "HOG". Carries a total of 48 rockets. Phan Thiet, South Vietnam, 1966.

OH-13 shot down north of Phan Thiet. Lt. Durling was able to make a crash landing despite his wounded friend being slumped over the controls. 1966.

Extracting troops from rice paddies north of Bong Son, South Vietnam. February, 1967.

Warrant Officers Erickson and Sisk on a landing zone in the dense jungle of An Lao valley, South Vietnam. April, 1967.

Captured ammo and weapons. Central Highlands, South Vietnam. Early, 1967.

Medevac jungle penetration pod. Bong Son, South Vietnam.

Major Blanton's (Wagonwheel Six) helicopter being washed in the An Lao river. Bong Son, South Vietnam. February, 1967. Crewchiefs Johnson and Wyatt.

Warrant Officer Sisk holding a piece of schrapnel that came through his tent and destroyed his lounge chair. April, 1967.

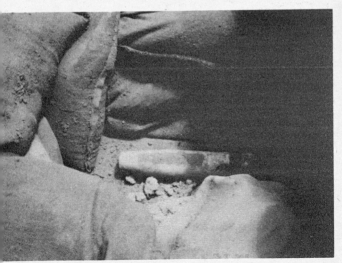

Unexploded motar round that landed just outside Warrant Officer Sisk's tent. April, 1967.

GENERAL ORDERS
NUMBER   6166

8 October 1967

AWARD OF THE DISTINGUISHED FLYING CROSS

1. TC 320. The following AWARD is announced.

SISK, ROBERT W. W3153325 WARRANT OFFICER W-1 United States Army
Company C, 229th Aviation Battalion (Assault Helicopter)

Awarded: Distinguished Flying Cross
Date action: 18 May 1967
Theater: Republic of Vietnam
Reason: For extraordinary heroism and gallantry while participating in aerial
           flight. Warrant Officer Sisk distinguished himself by heroism in
           action on 18 May 1967, while serving as aircraft commender of a UH-1D
           helicopter during a combat assault and extraction mission in the Re-
           public of Vietnam. During a hazardous mission into a booby trapped
           landing zone where several casualties already had been sustained when
           another aircraft detonated an enemy mine, Warrant Officer Sisk, dis-
           regarding his own safety, directed his aircraft in making a safe land-
           ing. He then directed the quick and successful extraction of the cas-
           ualties and the infantry troops. During the operation, Warrant Office
           Sisk made several safe landings into the booby trapped landing zone
           and contributed greatly to the success of the mission. His display of
           personal bravery and devotion to duty is in keeping with the highest
           traditions of the military service, and reflects great credit upon him
           self, his unit, and the United States Army.
Authority: By direction of the President, under the provisions of the Act of
           Congress, approved 2 July 1926.

        FOR THE COMMANDER:

OFFICIAL: GEORGE W. CASEY
                                           Colonel, GS
                                           Chief of Staff

DONALD W. CONNELLY
LTC, AGC
Adjutant General

15

The Horrors of War

We had been in Phan Thiet almost five months. Everyone was surprised when we received orders to return to An Khe.

I had begun to feel fairly comfortable at Phan Thiet despite the mortar and ground attacks. We had found ways to enjoy ourselves, somewhat. I had enjoyed the swimming in the ocean. We always went to the beach in groups. Usually we took a M60 machinegun plus individual weapons. One person stood guard while everyone else swam.

I quit going to the beach after Clyde was attacked by a sea snake one day.

Our company had also set up an overnight incountry R&R to Vung Tau. Supposedly, Vung Tau was an area where you were relatively safe. An undeclared truce with the Viet

Cong also was supposed to exist. They even had their own beach area, it was said.

This may have been true. We were told that we couldn't carry any weapons while in town. This alone would indicate that the town was safe. Being members of the 1st Air Cavalry and having been shot at more than once, made most of us reluctant to go anywhere without our weapons, however.

My turn came to go to Vung Tau. Reggie Morse was the other pilot going. Two of the enlisted crew rode along as gunners. The way the R&R worked, was that a crew would fly a helicopter down to Vung Tau and the crew already down there would fly it back to Phan Thiet.

Arriving in Vung Tau, I pulled my Smith & Wesson thirty-eight out of the holster and stuck the revolver in my waistband and pulled my jungle shirt back down over it. The other crewman did the same.

We hitched a ride into town. Reggie went to find some film for his camera. The two gunners and I went into the first bar we came to. This bar was like a thousand others I'd been into, from Nogales to Hong Kong. They all looked alike. The Bar Girls would give you a quick look-over as you walked through the door. This place was no different. We found a table and sat down. After ordering, three of the bar girls moved in. One of them sat down on my lap. She was cute until she opened her mouth. "Buy me one drink, honey," she said. The same old line, world wide. She had one tooth missing and her breath smelled like she had just devoured a rotten fish. "Beat it," I replied, pushing her off my lap.

"Cheapie skate GI Cheap Charlie sun-a-bitchy," she mumbled, again using the universal bar girl language.

As soon as she left, another one moved in. I turned three more away, feeling the verbal wrath of each one. The two crewmen sitting with me were having a good time. They had liked the first two girls that had sat down with them. They had bought them drinks and were getting along nicely.

The Navy SEALs had left their calling card. Evidently this joint was one of their hangouts when they were on liberty. Utilizing one whole wall, they had scrawled the Biblical passage about the valley of death, revising it somewhat. "I shall fear no evil, because I'm the meanest S.O.B. in the valley," it concluded.

I had been eyeballing the girl tending the bar. She appeared to be a little more ladylike, unlike the other girls. She had the "Dragon Lady" appearance. The tight-fitting silk dress with slits up both sides. Her hair was rolled into a bun with the stick thing running through it.

I moved over to the bar and ordered another beer. She opened the beer and set it before me. "You don't like any of my girls?" she asked.

"No," I replied. "I'd rather talk to a beautiful lady, like you." She smiled at the compliment. Her English was good, giving me the impression that she was well educated.

As the evening passed, I found out that she was co-owner of the establishment and at one time had been married to an officer in the French Army. She had lived in France for a while but had divorced her husband and returned to Vietnam.

It was getting late. A midnight curfew was in effect in Vung Tau. The place was deserted of customers. A few of the bar girls were straightening the tables and chairs.

"Where are you staying? You must leave now," the bar lady said, not waiting for my answer.

"I don't have a place to stay," I lied. I knew that Morse probably had a room at the Grand Hotel. I had told him I would meet him back there later.

"You can stay in one of the rooms out back, then. If you leave now the MPs will get you," she added.

She locked the front door then took all the money out of

the cash register, stuffing it into a canvas bag. We left through the back door where she paused to padlock it. We crossed a small courtyard and entered a neat-appearing, low-lying structure. She led me down a long hallway. On one side of the hall were doors leading to rooms where the bar girls lived, I deducted. At the end of the hall she removed a key from her purse and opened the door. The room was beautifully decorated and immaculately clean.

"Stay here until I find an empty room for you," she instructed as she turned and left, still clutching the bag of money. I was disappointed. I had figured I would be staying with her since she had brought me to her apartment. Oh well, to hell with it, I thought. I lay down on the bed to wait her return. I pulled the thirty-eight out from under my shirt and placed it under the pillow my head was resting on. I left my hand under the pillow next to the revolver.

I don't know how long I had been lying there, but I was on the verge of dozing off when I heard the door squeak. Someone was trying to open the door quietly. I guessed it to be the dragon lady. I thought if she saw I was asleep that she would just leave me there. I couldn't resist cracking my eyelids, however, and taking a peek through squinted eyes to see what she was doing.

I was startled to see two men creeping toward me. As near as I could tell, one appeared to be quite young, about sixteen or seventeen, I estimated. The other one was a little older, with a Ho Chi Minh–style goatee. The young one clutched a knife and was advancing toward me silently.

I sat up suddenly, flinging the pillow at the knife. In the same movement, I grabbed for the revolver. The sudden maneuver had surprised the intruders. They stood frozen, momentarily, in disbelief. I leveled the pistol toward them. The young one dropped the knife, turned and clawed his way over the other man who had fallen off balance. I fired just as both of them reached the door. They continued through the door. I fired again. I heard a loud scream from down the hall. The two men had disappeared. I jumped off the bed and moved cautiously toward the door with the thirty-eight cocked and pointing at the hallway. Wisps of smoke from the weapon drifted lazily around the dimly lit table lamp.

Doors along the hallway began opening and heads were peering cautiously about. "What in the hell is going on?" someone shouted. I recognized the voice of one of the gunners.

"Two dink bastards just tried to punch my ticket with a knife," I shouted back.

"That you, Mr. Sisk?" he asked.

"Right," I answered. The gunner emerged from a room half way down the hall. He stood there in his shorts holding his revolver in a ready position. His buddy appeared from a room across the hall. Their girls peered silently from the doorways.

"You must have hit one of them. I heard a scream," said the gunner.

"I don't know. They were hauling ass. I think I just scared the hell out of them." Just then four military policemen burst through the door with drawn weapons. The dragon lady trailed them.

I explained to them what had happened and showed them the knife. It was still lying where the intruder had dropped it.

"What are you doing carrying a weapon in Vung Tau, Sir?" the MP wanted to know.

"Division policy, Sergeant. Norton says we are to carry our weapons at all times," I replied, hoping General Norton of the 1st Air Cavalry had said that.

The MPs searched the building and the premises. As I

expected, they found nothing. They left with a warning not to bring any more weapons to town.

Everyone returned to their rooms. The dragon lady and I were alone in the hall. She was visibly shaken over the ordeal. Her voice quavered as she spoke. "I have a room down the hall for you. I am deeply sorry for what has happened."

She led me to the room, turned the covers down and fluffed the pillows. "Is there anything I can get for you?" she asked.

"Well, my throat is dry and I'm a little shaken. I guess I could use a cold beer," I said. She turned and left. Here we go again, I thought, as I stuck the thirty-eight under the pillow. I flipped the light off, undressed and got into bed. I didn't need another beer anyway, I thought.

A few minutes later there was a light rap on the door. "It is I," she said softly as she entered the room. "I have your beer."

A shaft of moonlight broke the otherwise darkened room. She set the beer on the night table and unzipped her dress. Letting the dress slide to the floor, she slipped under the covers and pressed her lips to my ear. "I want to apologize for all the trouble," she whispered.

"Oh what the hell, accept her apology, Buz," I said to myself. I covered my mouth with the back of my hand, shielding the stupid grin spread across my face.

16

The Super Assault

It was the beginning of the year, 1967. An Khe, the main camp of the 1st Air Cavalry was to be our new home.

I had spent very little time at An Khe. I was there briefly when I first arrived in Vietnam. A lot of my clothes and personal belongings were still in the tent I had been living in. Everything was mildewed. The heavy torrential rains kept everything damp and moldy.

Living at An Khe was relaxing compared to Phan Thiet. The flying consisted mostly of "ash-and trash" missions. This was the pilots' terminology for resupply and non-assault type flying. We were also responsible for flying the Infantry Ready Reaction Force if something did happen around An Khe.

Our respite was short lived. In less than two weeks of our

arrival back at An Khe, we were again told to pack for immediate deployment. Our destination this time would be Bong Son, a small hamlet northeast of An Khe. Operation "Thayer II" was in progress and we were needed to participate in the division-wide action.

All sixteen assault helicopters lifted from the "gold course" and in less than an hour we were breaking formation and landing at LZ English, the name given the camp at Bong Son. The camp was named after Specialist Five Carver J. English, killed in the crash of a CH-54 flying crane helicopter.

Our living area was located almost in the center of the camp. This was good for security reasons but our area had a drainage ditch running through the center of it. I could see problems when the heavy rains hit. The parking area for the helicopters was on a rounded hill just west of our living area.

The flying out of this landing zone would be over a combination of heavy, triple canopy jungle, mostly in the An Lao Valley area and flat rice paddy terrain on the Bong Son Plain.

All in all, over sixty "slicks" would be taking part in the assault. This would be a new first for the 1st Air Cavalry. Never before had such a large number of helicopters made such a large assault. The place we were going to hit was a fairly large village right on the coast, about thirty miles northeast of Bong Son. The landing zone would be the beach. This would make it a good LZ. There shouldn't be too many obstacles. The time in and out should also be at a minimum.

0400 on the morning of the assault, we were sitting in the helicopters with the engines running at idle. A radio check was made by Major Blanton, our flight leader. All aircraft commanders reported in that their aircraft was OK and they were ready to go.

"Wagonwheel Flight lifting," Blanton radioed. The plan was to fly the short distance to LZ Two Bits, just south of LZ English and pick up the troopers, we departed Two Bits and turned eastbound. We were to join up with the rest of the assault force just off the coast. As we approached the rendezvous area, I could see formations of helicopters orbiting out over the ocean.

"Stacked Deck Leader, Wagonwheel Flight approaching the coast," Blanton announced over the UHF radio.

"Roger that, Wheel Six. Fall in behind Bravo Flight. You should be able to see us. We're in a right orbit," responded Colonel Blair.

We were at two thousand feet. It was raining lightly with scattered grayish clouds at different altitudes. "Scud" we called it. Visibility wasn't that bad, but with the hordes of helicopters cramming the skies, all of the flight crews were more alert than usual.

The "Stacked Deck" Battalion turned north and flew up the coast where the 227th Assault Helicopter Battalion was forming up.

This was going to be quite an operation. The Navy was going to prep the area for us prior to the air assault. They had several destroyers lying off the coast.

The Air Force was providing a FAC aircraft and several F-100's. We also had our regular complement of Huey gunships and Aerial Rocket Artillery Helicopters. Two Chinook helicopters had been rigged as gunships. They were fitted with grenade launchers, rocket pods and fifty caliber machineguns.

Our flight joined up with the 227th and the massive helicopter assault force flew steadily northward.

We were getting close to the landing zone. I could see the

silhouette of one of the destroyers. Small flashes of light were flickering from the ship. The landing zone was being pounded by the destroyer's five-inch guns.

"I want two helicopter platoons landing at a time, trail formation. Keep the formations tight; I don't want my men scattered too thin along the beach," came the order from the Charlie-Charlie ship.

Eight helicopters would be landing at a time. The number of enemy that had taken over the village was unknown, but the estimate was that it could be a full battalion of NVA.

"The last volley of naval gunfire on the way," said the voice from the CC helicopter. "Last round on the ground" he said several seconds later.

My helicopter was the fourth ship in the second platoon, thus making me number eight in the Wagonwheel flight. We were close to the tail end of the whole assault force. I couldn't see the landing zone yet, but by the excited chatter on the radio I could tell that the first helicopters were landing their troops. The ARA helicopters and the gunships were attacking the village and reporting heavy ground fire.

"Wagonwheel Flight go trail formation," said Blanton. We had been flying diamond formations in order to keep everyone from straggling too much.

I dropped back and rolled in behind the third helicopter of our platoon; flying tucked in close and slightly higher than the ship in front of me. This allowed us to stay out of the rotor wash and exhaust of the aircraft ahead of us.

After going trail formation, I noticed that our platoon had dropped back at least a hundred yards behind Major Blanton's platoon.

"What in the hell is he doing now?" asked Klatskin, my co-pilot, quoting my thoughts exactly. This spacing would have been perfect for a four-helicopter LZ, but we were supposed to go in eight at a time.

"If Blanton finds out, he's going to chew ass" Brown, the gunner, piped in. The platoon leader wasn't thought of too well by the other crewmen in the platoon. He never liked flying in combat and wouldn't fly all that much on ash-and-trash missions either.

We were on final to the beach. The helicopters that had already dropped off their troops had made a right turn after climb out and were heading south out over the ocean.

As if suddenly remembering that he was supposed to land with the first four helicopters of our flight, our platoon leader nosed his helicopter over-trying to catch up. By this time we were on short final and quite close to the beach. We had already decided where our touchdown point would be but the sudden acceleration by our platoon leader screwed us all up. Everyone else accelerated also, not wanting to drop behind. I could anticipate what was going to happen. The platoon leader was going to make a run-on landing and try to close the gap while the first platoon discharged their troops.

The major problem with a run-on landing was that the beach sloped down toward the water. This would require touching down with the left skid and then slowly and smoothly lowering the collective and adding left cyclic stick simultaneously in order to get the right skid down. At the same time the helicopter had to be pointed straight ahead by manipulating the foot pedals. This was a maneuver that could be done, but required a great deal of skill. Under the conditions of being under fire and in formation, it was extremely dangerous.

At the last moment I decided to move my helicopter to the left of the one in front of me. My reasoning was that I wouldn't crash into the ship in front of me if something happened and I couldn't stop in time.

My decision proved to be a wise one. As the left skid of the helicopter in front of me touched down, a high arching rooster tail of sand rose and fell harmlessly to my right side. The same thing was happening to the other helicopters. The second and third helicopters had not moved to the side, however, and the full force of the sand blasted into their windshields and into the intakes of the turbine engines.

Just prior to touchdown, I had glanced at the airspeed indicator. We were showing almost forty knots. "I don't believe this stupid bastard," I muttered over the intercom. "He's trying to kill us all."

Our gunners were ordered not to fire after touchdown. The soldiers that had been helicoptered in just before us, were huddled down behind a three-foot sand dune between the landing area and the village. They were drawing heavy fire. Tracers were streaming in front of me and just behind the tail boom of the ship in front of me. Another problem cropped up. In their hurry to get off the helicopters, the troopers began jumping from the skids while the ships were still moving. A grunt from the ship in front of me slipped off the skid and the barrel of the machinegun mounted on the helicopter hit him in the side, spinning him around. He fell just as the tail rotor passed harmlessly over him.

The helicopters came to a stop. I had decided to hold in power and was holding the helicopter at a hover with just the left skid touching the sand. Our platoon leader had bottomed the collective and slammed the helicopter onto the beach. He slid sideways and had stopped only a few inches from the tail rotor of Blanton's Number Four ship. The other pilots were doing the same thing I was doing, holding power.

Huge columns of smoke billowed from the burning village. "Guns a go-go"—the CH-47 Chinooks converted to gunships were making runs on a tree line between our soldiers and the burning village.

As the second guns a go-go pulled up, a huge explosion erupted near the tree line. The gunships must have hit an enemy ammo dump.

We lifted off the beach. The concussion from the blast rattled my helicopter and moved us sideways. I saw a full-size palm tree hurled high into the air. It did a slow somersault and settled almost lazily upright in the center of a burning hootch. The tree stood proudly momentarily then the flames leapt skyward, crumbling the palm fronds into ash.

A scout helicopter reported the enemy retreating out of the village to the west.

"Why in the hell don't they let those zoomies drop a jelly sandwich on them," I said.

"You're transmitting," said Klatskin. I thought that I was talking on intercom but I had been talking over the air.

As if heeding my advice, the Infantry Commander contacted the Forward Air Controller. "Whiplash, you still got your boys on station?"

"Roger that, Sir. Where and what do you want?"

"Put all the napalm on the west side of the village. If the bastards want to escape that way, they better learn to walk on fire. The rest of the stuff can go on the village. My troops are all on the east side, along the sand berm. All the helicopters will be clear in a minute."

The F-100's roared in from north to south. The napalm canisters tumbled end over end and splattered the west edge of the village. The searing fire forced its way through the boiling black smoke. The intense heat and fire consumed everything, including the oxygen. Enemy soldiers caught in the area died either by the fire itself or by suffocation.

The massive helicopter assault had been a success. No helicopters were lost during the action, although several had taken hits from ground fire.

The planning and coordination for the operation had paid off. In the weeks to come, several more "super" air assaults would be conducted successfully.

17

R and R

I had been in Vietnam almost seven months. My turn for R&R was coming up so I decided to take my seven days in Bangkok, Thailand.

I caught a helicopter ride back to An Khe and tried to gather up a decent uniform out of all my mildewed clothes. Even the leather in my dress shoes was starting to rot.

The next leg of my trip was from An Khe to Cam Rhan Bay via an Air Force C-130. After spending a day at Cam Rhan, I finally boarded a Pan Am four-engine, prop plane. Shortly after lift-off and almost over Saigon, I was looking out through the window when one of the propellers on the starboard side began to slow and then came to a full stop.

As the pilots feathered the prop, a stewardess announced that there was a slight problem and we would be landing in Saigon in a few minutes.

I wasn't too concerned about the problem but was worried about getting stuck in Saigon and having my seven days rest and relaxation cut short.

After landing, we were allowed to disembark the airplane. Evidently the problem was not too serious. The pilots were getting a fluctuation in oil pressure and had decided to shut the engine down as a precautionary measure.

I went into the lounge and had a couple of beers while waiting for the plane to be checked out.

I was amazed at the number of people coming and going through the airport. Besides the hundreds of people in uniform, there were just as many in civilian clothes.

My seven months in Vietnam had dealt only with the war. I had forgotten that other aspects of life go on, even in a country deeply involved in a war.

I felt uneasy as I sat watching this hurried activity. Saigon had been the target of dozens of bombings, including the air terminal. I looked suspiciously toward any Asian carrying a satchel or briefcase. I was relieved when they called our flight to reboard the airplane.

The first night in Bangkok was like removing a heavy weight from around my neck. For the first time in a long time, I felt completely at ease. No worries about getting shot or blown up.

After arriving at my hotel, I couldn't wait to get to my room and take a shower. I was going to let the water run on me until I couldn't stand it any longer. A shower in the 1st Cavalry consisted of packing water in five gallon cans, carrying them up a ladder and dumping the water in a drum. Then you would crawl back down, undress and turn a valve on to let the water flow. There was no such thing as hot water.

After my shower, I decided to rest for a couple of hours before going out to dinner. I was looking forward to having a good time at a nice restaurant and then hitting the night clubs. My thoughts were also on the beautiful Thai women that seemed to be everywhere I looked.

I felt good as I stretched out on the bed. I had forgotten how nice a soft clean bed could feel. It was almost six PM, I planned to rest until about eight.

I must have fallen into a deep slumber immediately. The rattling of the door knob woke me. I bolted up into a sitting position, sweating and shaking. I couldn't figure out where I was in the darkness. I felt under the pillow for my revolver, becoming panicky when I didn't find it.

The door opened slowly, the room lightened and it came back to me where I was.

"Excuse me, Sir. Do you want your room made up?" the girl standing in the doorway asked.

I looked at my watch. It was almost ten thirty. "Damn," I said out loud. I had been sleeping four and a half hours.

"Why do you want to make up the room this time of night?" I asked.

The girl looked puzzled. "I'll come back later, Sir," she said, closing the door.

I turned on the bedside lamp and got out of bed. I began dressing hurriedly. I'll skip dinner because it's so late, I thought. I'll just go night clubbing.

I pulled back the heavy window curtains and sunlight flooded the room. I was astonished. "What in the hell is going on?" I questioned myself. I checked my watch again. It was running. Ten thirty-five, it said. I called the hotel front desk. "What time is it?" I asked.

"About ten thirty, Sir," came the reply. "Day or night?" I asked.

"Uh, daytime, Sir. Are you all right, Sir?" the clerk asked in a concerned tone.

"Yeah, I guess I slept a little longer than I thought," I

said, hanging up. I couldn't believe it! I had slept around the clock, sixteen and a half hours altogether!

The following six days went by rapidly. I spent the time sightseeing by day and going to the night clubs at night.

All too soon my R&R was over. I dreaded going back. I didn't want to leave Bangkok.

I rejoined my unit in Bong Son, enduring the kidding all R&R returnees went through. Most of the jokes were about the seven-day waiting period concerning venereal disease. My seven days passed; I breathed a little easier.

While I was gone, the 1st Cavalry had gone back into the An Lao Valley. This valley was used heavily by the NVA and Viet Cong forces. They moved troops and supplies along the trails leading down from the mountains of the central highlands. The An Lao River was also a favorite way to move men and equipment out of the valley and into the southern end of the Bong Son plain.

We had just resupplied a unit at the northern end of the valley. As we flew southward, gaining altitude, a Mayday came over the radio. I recognized "Yogi" Bair's voice. I knew that he was somewhere down the valley. We had left LZ English at the same time. Both helicopters were carrying supplies for units in the An Lao Valley. Bair was to pick up two KIA's after dropping off his supplies.

"What's the problem, Yogi?" I called over the radio. "I've lost tail rotor control. I'm in autorotation," Bair replied.

"OK, I'm looking for you. I'm southbound at this time," I said. My crew and I searched frantically for the descending helicopter.

"I've got him. Eleven o'clock, below us," said Johnson.

"We've got you, Yogi. I'll be landing behind you," I radioed.

"This is Headhunter Six," another voice broke in. "We're

just above you guys. I've got a flight of "Blues" I can land if you need them," added Headhunter.

The Blues were the Rifle Platoon of the famed 1st Squadron, 9th Cavalry. "Roger that, bring 'em down," said Bair.

Bair was trying to make it to a small rice paddy. A helicopter with a loss of tail rotor control will try to spin in the opposite direction of the main rotor if power is not decreased. To stop the aircraft from spinning, the collective control is lowered, relieving the power to the main rotor system. At the same time the aircraft enters autorotation.

Yogi made it to the clearing. As he pulled power back in to slow the rate of descent, the helicopter spun sharply to the right. The tailboom hit a dike running through the rice paddy and sheared off just behind the main fuselage. The helicopter hit sideways, teetered up on one skid and came to rest upright. One of the body bags containing a KIA, had shot out of the open door of the Huey and was lying thirty feet from the helicopter.

I landed just behind the damaged helicopter. The five slicks carrying the Blues, landed on all sides of the rice paddy. The infantrymen had a perimeter set up before Bair and his crew were out of the helicopter. Two gunships from the 1st of the 9th, roared low level down the sides of the rice paddy, looking for any enemy activity.

"Headhunter Flight lifting," Headhunter Six said. "I'll call this in as soon as I get some altitude," he added.

"OK, you might tell them to get a Chinook with a rigging crew headed this way. They'll have to sling the helicopter out," I answered.

We loaded the body bags into my helicopter. Bair and his crew pulled the machine guns off their helicopter. I flew the KIA's and the downed airmen back to Bong Son.

Several hours later, a Chinook brought the wrecked helicopter back to our landing area. The infantrymen of the Blue Team were picked up by their helicopters and returned to their base.

While looking Bair's helicopter over, it was discovered that a single bullet had hit the tail rotor drive shaft at such an angle that it sheared the shaft causing the tail rotor failure.

18

Black Bags of Death

The town of Quin Nhon lay along the South China Sea coast about sixty air miles southeast of Bong Son. Every night, about half of our helicopters were deployed from Bong Son to Quin Nhon. The reasoning being that if there was an attack on our base all of our helicopters would not be destroyed.

It wasn't a bad deal. We would alternate taking the helicopters to Quin Nhon and this would allow each crew to go about every third night. The bad thing was the flying all day and way up into the night and then having to fly to Quin Nhon. Many times we wouldn't get there until midnight or after. We would also have to leave around 0430 the following morning in order to get back to Bong Son in time for the early morning assaults.

Some of the advantages, however, made up for the lack

of sleep and inconvenience we experienced. A U.S. Army hospital was located at Quin Nhon, where a large number of nurses and doctors were stationed. They had a very nice officers' club that we were allowed to patronize. It soon got to the point where 1st Cavalry pilots were more in the club than medical personnel.

I arrived back at LZ English around 2200 after flying air assaults and hauling ammunition all day.

Captain May called on the radio from the operations tent and told me to refuel and then go to Quin Nhon. He also advised me that they were sending our dinners out to the helicopter and that we could eat enroute to Quin Nhon. This was not unusual as we often ate our meals while flying. May told me that I was to fly over to the east side of the camp and pick up two KIA's before going to Quin Nhon. This was the unpleasant part of the trip.

Every night, the helicopters dispatched to Quin Nhon would pick up the American soldiers that had been killed in action that day and transport them there where they would eventually be transferred to the huge morgue in Saigon.

I always felt uneasy when I flew the KIA's. I had seen many people killed and wounded but there was something about the black body bags that made me feel uneasy.

When I first started transporting the dead Americans, I would read the green tags attached to the bags. The tags would give name, rank, age, and usually the type of wounds the soldier had died from. I think reading the tags was what made me feel uncomfortable.

I couldn't help thinking about the dead soldiers' families somewhere back home. There were probably prayers being said for the safety of those men even as they lay dead on the hard floor of a helicopter. I was sure that the mothers, wives and children would not know of their loved one's fate for several days after they had been killed.

I landed at the location to pick up the KIA's; I saw the body bags in the glare of the landing lights. Several soldiers sat on the fenders of a Jeep smoking and shielding their eyes from the blowing sand and dust that we had stirred up. The soldiers waited patiently as the crewchief and gunner worked hurriedly to unlatch the troops seats and fold them against the bulkhead.

The co-pilot had been holding the paper plates containing our dinners. I reached over for mine and began eating.

"How in the hell can you eat with dead guys lying in the back?" the co-pilot asked. He was new in the country having been in 'Nam less than two weeks. It was also his first time carrying KIA's.

"It doesn't make a damn," I said. "You'll find out that you will get hungry no matter how many dead people you see."

"Well, I can't eat right now."

"OK, you fly then. I'll finish my supper."

The crewchief and gunner slid the KIA's into the helicopter. They unfastened the M60's from their mounts and laid the machineguns under their seats. "We're up," the crewchief shouted as he slid the Huey's door shut.

The co-pilot lifted the helicopter to a hover and received clearance from the tower to depart to the south. I called our operations center and told the sergeant on duty that we were enroute to Quin Nhon.

"Roger, Sir. Give me a call when you have a talley ho on the airfield," he answered.

The flight was uneventful. We cruised at five thousand feet. This put us out of the range of fire from the Bad Guys and would also give us range for radio communications. I spotted the runway lights at Quin Nhon and radioed operations that we had the airfield in sight. I called the tower and we received clearance to land. I advised the tower that we had KIA's on board and requested the appropriate people be there to pick them up.

We landed at the parking ramp. There was no sign of the Graves and Registration people. I called the tower again and they assured me that they had contacted the G. and R. people and that they should be there shortly.

We waited outside the helicopter. I was anxious to get to the club. The crewchief and gunner hadn't had dinner yet. They didn't want to eat while flying. They had planned on a real civilized meal at the enlisted men's club.

"You guys go ahead and take off," I told them. "I'll wait for them to pick up the KIA's. I'll see you here at 0430. Don't get thrown in jail," I added jokingly.

I lit up a cigar and sat down on the ramp. The co-pilot had his flashlight on and was reading the green tag on one of the body bags.

"This guy was only nineteen," he said, breaking the silence. "Sez here he died from fragment wounds, upper body. Think I'll take a look."

"I don't think you want to do that," I said. I never had the desire to unzip a body bag for a look. I felt that it was too disrespectful.

"Aw, it won't hurt anything. Besides, I've been here almost two weeks and haven't seen any dead people yet."

He unzipped the bag. As he pulled the material apart, he let out a blood curdling scream and leaped backwards. The soldier's head had been severed. It must have been resting on the chest of the body. As the co-pilot opened the bag, the head rolled out onto the floor of the helicopter and then dropped out onto the ground, hitting the helicopter skid as it fell. It rolled past me and came to rest about eight feet from the helicopter.

I sat there stunned. The co-pilot was bent over, by the front of the helicopter, vomiting his guts out.

Just then a truck pulled up. I could see the severed head illuminated by the headlights of the truck. The face was caked with dried blood and dirt that had turned pinkish from the blood.

"What in the fuck is going on?" one of the soldiers asked as he got out of the truck.

I got up and walked over the soldier. "We started to pull the body bag out for you guys and I guess the zipper was broken or undone. This guy's head rolled out and scared the crap out of us," I lied.

"No problem," said the soldier. He walked over and picked the head up, one hand over each ear. He carried the head as casually as if he had just picked a pumpkin from the patch. He put it back in the body bag and zipped it shut. The soldiers loaded the KIA's in the truck and left.

The co-pilot had quit throwing up. He remained silent. We walked the half mile to the officers club and didn't quit drinking until the club closed.

19

The Rain of Death

"Fly your helicopter down to LZ Two Bits to be fitted with a tank and spray booms," Captain May explained to me.

I had sprayed many of the surrounding camps and fire bases for mosquitoes before. I figured it would be more of the same.

I landed at Two Bits. My crew and the spray people began to slide the huge tank inside the helicopter. The long boom was attached to the skids and hoses were connected from the tank to the spray boom.

As the crew fastened the equipment into place, a captain carrying a map walked over to me and asked if I was the aircraft commander. "Yes, I am," I replied.

"These are the areas we want sprayed," he said, pointing to some markings he had made on the map.

"There are no camps or firebases in these areas," I said, examining his map and comparing it to my own. "Why do you want to spray for mosquitoes in these areas?"

"We're not spraying for mosquitoes. Intelligence has determined that the rice paddies in those locations are being cultivated and harvested by the Viet Cong. We've got orders to spray them and kill the rice before they can harvest any more of it."

The crew of men began pumping the liquid out of fifty-five-gallon barrels and into the tank.

As the tank began to fill, a valve at the bottom of the tank began to leak. The valve controlled the flow of liquid to the boom. I had no way of operating the valve from the cockpit. A crew member had to sit by the valve and would turn it on or off on my command.

"This valve is leaking," I said as I made a swipe through the liquid with my fingers. The spray was dripping onto the floor of the helicopter and slowly trickling toward the open door.

"What is this shit, anyway?" I asked the captain. "Oh, it's just diesel oil and some other crap they use," he answered. It felt a little oily. I wiped my fingers on my jungle fatigue pants.

The crewchief tightened the valve with a wrench but it continued to drip.

We lifted off Two Bits and headed north. The captain was squatted down just behind the pilots' seats and in front of the huge tank.

We arrived over the area to be sprayed. I circled while the captain attempted to determine the paddies to be sprayed. I knew it was going to be a three-ring circus. The captain had the paddies marked on his map, but once we were over the area it was impossible to tell one paddy from the other.

"Do you see that field down there where that gook and the water buffalo are?" the intelligence officer asked.

"Roger," I replied.

"Let's start on that paddy and work north," he said.

"There isn't any rice growing in that field. That dink is plowing that area up," I said.

"I can't help it. That's one of the areas they want sprayed." I made a descending turn and lined up on the paddy. "Turn the valve on, Johnson," I said, as we approached the edge of the field. At the end of the paddy I pulled up sharply and did a pedal turn, dropping back down for the next swath.

The Vietnamese farmer had stopped plowing and was standing motionless, watching us as we worked our way toward him. He waved as I flew directly over him. At the end of the field I made another turn for the return run. The spray was still settling around the farmer as we passed him again. The helicopter's windshield was covered with the spray. There was no wind and the mist seemed to hang in the air.

We emptied the tank and headed back to Two Bits to reload. I turned the controls over to the co-pilot and looked back to see what the captain was doing. He had his flight helmet off and was vomiting in it.

"I guess the captain didn't like our crop dusting technique. He's puking his guts out," I said to the crew over the intercom.

"I don't feel so good myself," said Brown, the gunner. "I've never gotten airsick before. I think this fucking spray has something to do with it."

We landed at Two Bits to reload. The intelligence officer was still sick. He handed me the map and told me to spray the designated areas as I saw fit.

As we arrived back over the area, I could see some of the

rice we had sprayed earlier was already beginning to wilt. There was no sign of the Vietnamese farmer or his water buffalo.

Over the next several days, we sprayed hundreds of acres of rice. There was no way to determine the Good Guys from the Bad Guys. We sprayed everything in sight. The spray killed everything it touched.

Little did I know that years later, of the Americans who had survived the shooting war, many would fall victim to the chemical war. Almost all of it due to our own determination to deprive the enemy of food and concealment.

20

Charlie-Charlie

Besides providing a commander with an Airborne Command Post, other duties of the Charlie-Charlie helicopter included the recon of potential landing zones for future helicopter air assaults.

A Command and Control helicopter assigned to the 3rd Brigade, 1st Air Cavalry operating out of Landing Zone Two Bits was reconning a proposed site west of the An Lao Valley. The terrain was hilly and covered with heavy jungle growth.

As the aircraft made a pass over the small clearing, bullets ripped into the fuselage and engine compartment. The pilot began an immediate climb but a bullet had shattered a fuel line and the engine had flamed out. With all the communication equipment on the helicopter, the crew was able to transmit a Mayday distress call and their location.

The pilot put the helicopter into autorotation and made a 180-degree turn back into the same clearing they had just reconned. Because of the steep descent, the helicopter hit the ground hard, spreading the skids and flexing the main rotor blades down into the tail boom.

The crew and passengers, although shaken, were unhurt. They soon began receiving fire from the dense jungle just east of the downed helicopter. Machineguns were pulled from the aircraft and a defensive position set up behind a rotting log.

Wagonwheel Flight was on the east side of the An Lao valley, northbound. We were enroute to a landing zone with skytroopers of the 1st Battalion, 7th Cavalry.

Our operations radioed us to divert to the downed aircraft. They also advised that the crew was under attack and that we could expect heavy ground fire.

I was flying wingman to the flight leader. My co-pilot had been in country several weeks but had not participated in a "hot" combat assault.

We arrived over the downed aircraft and could see the fierce firefight going on. Our escort gunships peeled off from the formation and began suppressive firing runs on the enemy's position.

"I can see only one possible landing site" the flight leader said. "The little opening with the stream running through it. Everyone go trail formation. This will be a single ship LZ." I rolled in behind Yellow One and spaced myself about thirty seconds behind.

"Do you want to do the flying on this assault?" I asked Wyatt*, the co-pilot. He seemed fidgety and nervous.

"I guess so. I'll give it a try," he answered reluctantly.

---

* This name has been changed to protect the privacy of the individual involved.

"Just remember, concentrate on flying the aircraft. Keep your spacing. If you get too close to Yellow One, then you'll end up coming in too slow and we'll be a sitting target."

Yellow One rolled out on final and began his approach.

"We can't land. There is a tall snag in the middle of the LZ and big boulders in the stream bed," the flight leader radioed. His helicopter was hovering over the small clearing, the rotor blades just barely clearing the tall stump. A burst of tracer rounds sliced across the tail boom as the infantry troops began to drop onto the rocks and into the stream.

"Slow your rate of descent, Wyatt," I told my co-pilot. He didn't seem to respond. We were fast approaching the LZ and Yellow One was still inserting his troops. "Slow your rate of descend," I repeated. Yellow One lifted slowly up and out of the small hole in the jungle. By now our aircraft was descending rapidly and at a very steep angle.

"OK, I've got it," I said as I grabbed the controls. I couldn't budge them. I glanced over at Wyatt and he was sitting there staring straight ahead. He still had both hands locked on the controls. "Turn loose of the fucking controls," I screamed at him.

Wyatt was frozen on the controls. He seemed to be in a trance.

"He's going to splatter us, Sir," Johnson shouted over the intercom. By now the infantrymen could see what was happening. They didn't know whether to jump or to ride it out.

"Johnson, get up here and pull him loose." By now I was scared. I couldn't overpower Wyatt on the controls. Johnson was clawing his way forward over the grunts, frantically trying to get to Wyatt. I could see he wasn't going to make it. I removed my right hand from the stick and backhanded Wyatt in the throat with a karate chop. As his head snapped back, he released the controls and clutched his throat. I yanked the collective control up to the stops. The helicopter felt like it was flying apart as the blades grabbed for air trying to slow the descent. It seemed to stop momentarily and then, as the rotor r.p.m. drained off, settled toward the rocks in the stream bed. The grunts were jumping from both sides by this time and the loss of weight helped me gain a little control over the helicopter. I still couldn't get it to hover. As it settled, the blades smashed into the snag. Huge chunks of metal were ripped from the ends of the blades. Now, almost gently, the ship touched down on the rocks. I was able to balance it there as the rotor r.p.m. built back up. I was faced with a real dilemma. I could chance trying to fly the helicopter back out and hope that the blades would hold together, or stay where I was, thus blocking the only possible landing site and the rescue of the few of us on the ground.

"Yellow Three, short final," the aircraft commander of the next approaching helicopter announced.

I decided to go for it. I pulled in pitch. The helicopter vibrated violently but started lifting. I continued to pull power until we cleared the trees. As I nosed the ship over to gain forward airspeed, the helicopter began to shudder and vibrate much worse. I could not read the instrument panel because of the violent vibrations. The blades began to shuck more metal. I backed off on the airspeed and reduced the rotor r.p.m. to the very minimum flying r.p.m. I called Yellow One and told him what was going on.

"There is a fire base about six miles southeast," he said.

"Do you think that the thing will fly that far?" he asked in a concerned tone.

"I don't know, Sir. I can't read my gauges or my map." My voice sounded like someone had me by the shoulders and was shaking me violently.

The other helicopters had dropped off their sky troopers and were following behind me and Yellow One. I could only guess my airspeed. I couldn't be flying much more then twenty-five knots.

"If you get us down in one piece, I'll buy you all the beer you can drink and kiss your ass in downtown Saigon," Brown suddenly blurted over the intercom. Leave it to Tom Brown to take the edge off a tense situation.

"I'll take you up on all the beer I can drink, Tom, but after what I did in my pants back there I don't think you'll want to do the other." I laughed. Just the sound of our quavering voices was funny.

The flight leader led me to the fire base. I landed the helicopter and shut it down.

It was unbelievable that the helicopter would fly with so much blade damage. The snag had busted about twelve inches off each blade. We were fortunate that about an equal amount from each blade was gone. Had only one blade been shortened, the blades would have been so far out of balance that if I had tried to fly it, we would have crashed.

We got the co-pilot out of the cockpit. He still seemed dazed. He could not remember anything that happened after starting into the landing zone. He was later transferred to a maintenance unit where the only flying he had to do was test flights. I felt sorry for him but he had come close to killing us all.

Our maintenance officer flew a replacement helicopter out to me. After looking at my damaged ship, he wouldn't believe that I had flown it in that condition. They brought a new set of blades out to the fire base and changed them there.

The infantry had managed to drive the enemy off and they had also cleared a landing spot. The downed crewmen and passengers from the Charlie-Charlie ship were picked up and transported back to LZ Two Bits. After a Chinook helicopter and a rigging crew had recovered the CC helicopter, we went back in and extracted the infantrymen. The whole ordeal had lasted less than three hours.

Early the following morning, Surf Owen and his crew flew their helicopter down to Two Bits to get radios installed for a Charlie-Charlie ship. Our company was going to provide a CC helicopter until they received a replacement for the one that had been shot down.

Owen was reconning an area north of Bong Son on the Bong Son plain when they flushed about a dozen Viet Cong from along a stream bed. The Cong began firing at the helicopter. The door gunner returned the fire along with the first sergeant and the Battalion CO. They were firing their M16s on full auto. They killed two of the Cong, but during the gunfight Owen's helicopter took a bullet through the dog house, the cowling covering the engine. The bullet nicked an oil line and oil began spraying all over the hot turbine engine. Smoke began boiling out of the engine compartment and the engine oil gauge was showing a steady drop in pressure.

Owen made a forced landing at a South Vietnamese compound just as they lost all oil pressure. Maintenance personnel were flown out to the downed helicopter and repaired the oil line. This was the second Charlie-Charlie to be shot down in as many days.

Flying the CC ship was beginning to look more and more unattractive.

Owen flew the Charlie-Charlie helicopter the next several days. He was flying twelve to sixteen hours a day. Doug Clyde relieved Owen as Aircraft Commander. I went to fly as Clyde's co-pilot a few days later. Clyde's regular co-pilot was going on R&R.

We were orbiting high over a small village located in the northwest corner of the Bong Son plain, watching the helicopters from our company assault the village.

A scout helicopter from the 1st of the 9th Cavalry had spotted a large number of North Vietnamese regulars infiltrating into the village from the mountains just west of the town.

There was an American Artillery Fire Base about three quarters of a mile south of the village. The general consensus was that the enemy force was going to launch an attack on the fire base after darkness had set in.

The Battalion CO asked us to set him down on the small hill where the artillery firebase was located. We landed and shut the helicopter down. The colonel, his sergeant and the Battalion Artillery Officer grabbed their weapons and packs and started down the hill toward the village. We could hear the firing between our troops and the enemy.

"Wait here for us. If we're not back by dark, fly back to Bong Son and come back out first thing in the morning," the colonel shouted as he disappeared over the hill. He was going to join up with his men on the outskirts of the village and lead the assault on the North Vietnamese himself.

Clyde and I walked out to the highest point of the hill to watch the artillerymen blast the village with the 105 guns.

They had the guns suppressed and were firing point blank into the village. Every once in a while they would get a direct hit on a thatch house. The house would explode into bits and pieces and the burning material would be blown into other houses, setting them on fire.

I was sitting on a large rock watching the action. Clyde was squatted down just to my left, puffing on a cigarette. I estarted hearing noises like a bee would make zinging by your head. "Zzz-et, zz-et."

"Clyde, I think we're getting shot at," I said, not really wanting to believe it.

"Naw, I think we're out of range. I think it's just insects or bees or something," he said, still drawing on the cigarette. Just then a bullet smashed into the base of the rock, sending dirt and pieces of gravel flying. I fell backwards off the rock. Landing on the ground and scrambled on all fours for the backside of the hill. Clyde was already there, panting like a dog after a long chase.

It took several minutes to catch my breath. "If those were bees, that last son-of-a-bitch just had one hellava collision with that rock," I had to say sarcastically. We wandered back over to our helicopter and kept a low profile.

A half hour later, the 105 Howitzers ceased firing. The small arms and automatic weapons fire increased furiously. I chanced another look. I duck-waddled back to the rock and peered cautiously around it.

Our soldiers had risen from behind the small rice paddy dikes and were rushing the village.

Two helicopter gunships had arrived and were patrolling the northwest side of the village to keep the enemy from escaping to the foothills and mountains.

I could also see an OH-13 scout helicopter snooping around the outskirts of the village on the southwest side. The crazy bastard was hovering down below the tree line and trying to cave the thatch roof of one of the hootches in with the skids of the helicopter.

There was a sudden burst of an automatic. Unmistakably the deep, throaty rattle of an AK-47. The scout helicopter did a 180-degree spin over the hootch and began a laborious climb straight up.

As soon as the helicopter cleared the palm trees, it headed straight toward us. It was trailing smoke and I could hear the reciprocating engine cutting in and out. The nose of the ship would yaw from each loss and resurgence of power.

The scout helicopter made a run-on landing just to the left of our parked ship. As the helicopter skidded to a halt, the engine let out a huge bellow, backfired and quit. It was strangely quiet. The only noise was the swish, swish of the blades as they wound down and drifted to a halt.

The pilot was already outside the helicopter. He was busy pulling an M16 out of a rifle scabbard and inserting a clip into the rifle. He seemed totally indifferent to the damage his helicopter had sustained.

"That little rat bastard had been poppin' rounds at us all day," he said, as Clyde and I walked up to the helicopter. He was now busy stuffing hand grenades into the pockets of his jungle shirt. I couldn't believe all the crap they had on the little helicopter. The center seat held a small wooden box crammed full of hand grenades, rifle clips, smoke grenades and several boxes of .45 caliber shells.

"He's got me pissed. I'm gonna go down there and bust his cookies once and for all, now," he continued, as he released the slide on the .45 automatic.

The pilot was a chief warrant officer, W-2. If he would have had a pointed cowboy hat on, he would have been the spittin' image of Festus of the old *Gunsmoke* series. It looked like he hadn't shaved in several weeks. Four or five of his upper front teeth were missing. When he wasn't talking, his teeth were clenched shut and his tongue moved in and out through the gap left by the missing teeth. I'm sure he wasn't, but he looked to be fifty years old. Damn, he's ugly, I thought. I wasn't about to tell him, though.

The 1st Air Cavalry wasn't known for its "spit and polish" while in combat but this guy would have made the grimiest guy in the Cavalry look like a member of an Honor Guard.

There is no way of preflighting an OH-13 without getting a little greasy. This pilot looked as though he long ago quit using a grease rag and just started using his jungle fatigues to wipe his hands on. His clothes were shiny from the rubbed-in grease and oil. If he would have caught on fire, they would have had to bring in Red Adair to put him out.

The gunner/observer was quietly checking his weapons and stuffing grenades into his pockets, also. He appeared to be about nineteen. His clothes were a lot cleaner and he also seemed to be more soldierly.

"You ready, Jimmy? Let's go get the little mother-fucker," the warrant officer said, not giving Jimmy time to answer.

By this time some of the artillery men had ambled over to see what was going on.

"We can put a salvo into that hootch and blow it off the map, Chief," the artillery sergeant said.

"No, I'm going to scratch this Commie bastard myself. I've got him figured out. He's got a tunnel leading from inside that hootch to a spider hole about thirty yards west. When we first saw him, he was firing at us from the doorway of the hootch. While we were trying to punch a hole in the roof with the skids to drop a grenade in, the little slope bastard popped out of the spider hole and riddled us."

"How do you know it's the same dink?" I asked.

"He's got a yellow bandana tied around his neck. Probably one he took from the body of one of our own guys."

Without further comment they started down the hill. We watched them for the next half hour moving cautiously across the paddies, sometimes crawling, sometimes running in a low crouch. They reached the edge of the village and disappeared in a clump of bushes.

For lack of anything else to do, Clyde and I attempted to count the bullet holes in the little observation helicopter. We lost track after seventeen. There was no way of telling if the bullets or fragments had caused the holes in the plastic bubble. It was short of a miracle that neither crewman had been injured. One bullet had hit the M60 machinegun putting it out of action. The fact that the gunner was holding the gun and was not injured was a miracle in itself.

The sun had disappeared behind the mountains west of us. It had been several hours since the pilot and the gunner of the OH-13 had left for the village. It would be dark soon. We had heard nothing from the Battalion Commander. Clyde decided we would wait until last light and if the colonel didn't show by then, we would fly back to LZ English.

The battle in the village was still going on. The small arms fire had diminished somewhat but would increase dramatically whenever a helicopter would land in a paddy southeast of the village. Several "Dustoff" Medevac helicopters with the big Red Cross painted on the sides had been shuttling in and out, evacuating the wounded Americans. Several of our company's helicopters had also made several trips in bringing ammo and supplies.

Just as we were preparing to leave, we heard someone working their way up the hill. We could hear muffled voices. "Must be the colonel," said Clyde.

Five minutes later, the warrant officer topped the hill. His greasy fatigues were now covered with mud and slime from the rice paddies. His breathing came in gasps. He dropped to the ground and leaned back against the skid crosstube on our helicopter. With each gasp for air, his tongue would shoot out through the missing teeth gap. He reminded me of a snake trying to pinpoint his prey. The gunner flopped down beside the pilot.

After a few minutes, his breathing eased somewhat. "Got 'im," he said, not even looking up. "I don't know how far it is to Buddha land but that little son-of-a-bitch should be checkin' in 'bout now. Got me a souvenir, too," he added.

Carefully, as if he was about to display the Star of India, he pulled the blood-stained yellow bandana from the breast pocket of his jungle shirt. Delicately, he began to unfold the bandana. Inside were two blood-caked human ears. A cocklebur was stuck to the ear lobe of one of them.

The pilot looked up grinning, as if seeking approval.

The colonel never showed, so we lifted off for Bong Son. The OH-13 pilot asked us to drop him and his gunner off at Two Bits. On the way, he told us how they had stormed the hootch but didn't find the enemy soldier. The gunner began lobbing grenades in to the tunnel hole they had found concealed in the hootch. The pilot had crawled out to the spider hole and waited a few yards away, concealed behind a palm tree. The dust, smoke and concussions had finally driven the enemy soldier out of the tunnel and to the spider hole. When he eased his head out of the hole to take a look, the pilot had fired a whole magazine from his M16. The burst had killed the NVA soldier instantly.

We dropped the two airmen off at Two Bits and departed for LZ English. "I'm glad to get away from those two guys. They give me the creeps," stated Clyde.

"Be glad of one thing," I said.

"What's that?" Clyde asked.

"Be glad that they're on our side!"

21

One Day in May

For the first twenty-nine years of my life the eighteenth of May meant nothing to me except for being just another day.

I knew that people were born on the eighteenth of May, people died on that day; probably some significant occurrences even took place somewhere in history. But I didn't give a damn, it was just one more day to get through in 1967, another day of surviving.

Before the day was through, however, it would be a day etched into my memory, never to be erased. Eighteen, May, 1967 would be my Pearl Harbor, my "Remember the Alamo." For some of the other men involved in this small portion of the war, it would be the final day of their lives. For others it would be the beginning of a style of life feared and dreaded by all soldiers involved in combat. That of the maimed and crippled, the paralyzed; the helplessness of confinement to beds or wheelchairs until the day they died.

It was to be another routine, if you can call it that, combat assault. The small hill had been reconned and little if any resistance was expected. We were to air assault the hill, the infantrymen would secure it and then the artillery guns would be slung in, making the hill a fire base to support our troops operating in the area.

The hill was about fifteen miles north of the fire base where Clyde and I had been shot at a few weeks earlier. It was located in the farthest northwest corner of the Bong Son plain.

I was flying White Two, the sixth helicopter in the assault force. The LZ would not be prepped by artillery or ARA ships. If it had been, it would probably have prevented what was about to take place.

"Two Ship LZ," the flight leader announced. "Thirty-second intervals." The helicopter formations began breaking into twos and slowing to obtain proper spacing.

One of the escort gunships made a low-level pass over the LZ and dropped a red smoke grenade. The flight leader noted the wind direction from the drift of the smoke, turned back toward the east and rolled out on final to the LZ.

The Cavalrymen leaped from the open doors and squatted down behind the boulders and clumps of brush. Yellow One and Two lifted out of the LZ. Yellow Three and Four landed and discharged their soldiers. White One and my helicopter were next in. White One touched down on the northeast corner of the landing zone. I had to drop a little farther back and slightly behind White One in order to find a spot where I could get low enough to let my passengers off. I noticed a large rock just outside my left door. I was concentrating on setting the left skid beside the rock when a huge explosion ripped the LZ. "Son-of-a-Bitch," someone screamed over the radio. I didn't know if it was one of the pilots or one of the infantrymen on the Fox mike radio.

Three or four of the soldiers from White One had jumped out of the right door and were running, almost in a group, toward some boulders where some other soldiers were already taking cover. The explosion tore through them like a dust devil uprooting tumbleweeds. I sat watching in horror. Everything seemed to have been turned into slow motion. As the soldiers were lifted into the air, pieces of their bodies seemed to separate and drift away. Arms and legs floated around as if trying to find their owners. A chunk of torso slammed into my windshield, blotting out the Plexiglas with blood, bits of flesh and shattered bones. Shredded pieces of jungle fatigues clung to the windshield wipers.

"Dear God. Dear God," the co-pilot mumbled over and over. It seemed like we had been sitting there for hours watching some horrible ghoulish movie.

"White Three short final," the Aircraft Commander of the next two helicopters announced. His voice broke the trance or shock or whatever it was that had happened to me.

"Go around! Go around!" I shouted over the UHF. "The LZ is booby trapped!" I repeated several times.

"Get those fuckin' helicopters out of here! They're detonating the mines!" a hysterical voice was screaming over the FM radio.

"We've sustained aircraft damage but we are lifting out," the AC of White One said.

"White Two, are you up?"

"Negative," I replied. "I can't see through my windshield. I'll have to get it cleared. I think I have blade damage also but I'll fly it out as soon as I can see."

I turned the windshield wipers on hoping to clear the windshield enough for me to see. The wipers made things worse. They spread the blood and bits of flesh even more, smearing the windshield into a crimson blur. A long piece of intestine was hung up on one of the wipers and was being slapped back and forth across the windshield. I told the crewchief to grab the water jug we always carried and to dump it on the windshield. I turned the wipers off while the crewchief shuffled carefully along the skid to the front of the ship. Standing on the raised toe of the skid, he began wiping away the remains with his glove. He grabbed the intestine, ripped it from the wiper and threw it. He then started pouring the water from the top of the windshield. He hollered for me to turn the wiper back on. As the wiper started up it flung the mixture of water and blood, splattering the crewchief in the face and chest. He continued pouring the water. With each swipe of the blades, he would catch the full force of the water and remains in the face. Just as he poured the last of the water, the windshield cleared enough to see through.

The crewchief made his way aft, sliding along on top of the skid. Before pulling himself into the helicopter, he grabbed his jungle shirt at the bottom and ripped all of the buttons off. He then pulled his bloody flight gloves off and threw them down. He pulled his shirt off, tried to wipe his face with the tail of the shirt and then threw it on the ground. He wearily pulled himself up and into his seat. After plugging in his helmet cord, he said, "We're up." His voice was almost a whisper and sounded like the very tired last words of a dying man.

Several wounded men lay sprawled around the LZ. The other soldiers stood or squatted down, frozen in their tracks. Not knowing where the other booby traps were hidden, they were afraid to move or go to the aid of the wounded.

One soldier lay on his back, his knees drawn up, almost touching his chest. One arm was raised in a plea for help. There was no hand at the end of the upraised arm. A medic stood a short distance away, agonizing over whether to go to his aid or not. He started walking cautiously toward the wounded man. He couldn't have walked more than five steps when another explosion went off. The medic disappeared in a ball of orange flame and a dust cloud.

Thinking my helicopter had detonated the second booby trap, Yellow One, the flight leader screamed over the radio, "White Two, get the hell out of there!" Not bothering to answer or explain, I pulled pitch and lifted the helicopter straight up for about 150 feet so the rotor downwash would not trigger another explosion.

The Command and Control helicopter had already called back to LZ English for Dustoff helicopters and a bomb disposal team with mine detectors. To save time, the disposal team was riding out with the Medevac helicopters.

White One had landed in a dry rice paddy about a mile east of the LZ to check the damage to his ship. I dropped down and landed close by, but then hovered over to a small stream on the other side of the dike surrounding the rice paddy. One of Delta Company's gunships flew overhead covering us while we inspected the aircraft. The other gunship continued to circle the LZ providing support, if needed, for the men trapped on the LZ.

White One had sustained shrapnel damage to the tail boom and a couple of dents in the rotor blades. Outside of the mess created by the pieces of body, my helicopter had no damage.

The crewchief and gunner began dipping water out of the stream and throwing it over the front of the helicopter. Before long almost all signs of the blood and mess were gone with the exception of blood on the main rotor blades. We could not reach them to clean them off.

The crewchief went back to the stream and began splashing water on his face trying to remove the smeared blood that he hadn't been able to get off with his shirt tail. The gunner was washing the blood off the crewchief's flight helmet.

The commander in the CC helicopter decided to land the remaining soldiers still in the helicopters, in the rice paddy where we had landed. This would provide security for us and still have them close by the men still on the LZ.

Just as the rest of the helicopters landed in the paddy, two Dustoff helicopters showed up with the bomb team and extra medics. The Commander was trying to decide what the best course of action should be.

The platoon leader on the LZ was absolutely against landing the Dustoff helicopter on the LZ. The commander was trying to explain that the only way to get them out would be to fly the bomb disposal team in to clear a path for them. He was also concerned about the wounded who had been lying there for a half hour now. As near as they could tell, four soldiers had been killed and at least five wounded. The seriousness of the wounded could not be determined since no one was able to get to them.

"What we need is one helicopter that can land in the exact spot where they touched down originally," the Battalion CO said to the flight leader.

White One was damaged and already headed back to Bong Son. Out of the four helicopters of Yellow Flight, none of the pilots could be sure of their exact landing site.

"What about you, Sisk? Can you remember your landing site?" the flight leader asked.

"I'm certain I can," I replied. I told him about the one distinct rock that I had concentrated on, setting the left skid right next to it.

"Well, I'm not telling anyone to go back in there, but we have to get those soldiers out. It's strictly a volunteer flight," the flight leader said.

"No question about it, I'll go back in. I'm positive of my

landing site. My crew does not have to go if they don't want to." I told the flight leader what had taken place and the ordeal the crewchief had gone through.

When told they didn't have to fly back into the booby trapped LZ, the crewchief became very upset. "I go where my helicopter goes," he said angrily. The gunner and co-pilot simply stated that they would stick with the helicopter.

Three bomb disposal soldiers and five medics with their equipment loaded into the helicopter. We lifted off and headed back to the landing zone. I was nervous. My flight gloves were wet with perspiration. I had been confident I could find my original landing spot, but now I began to worry that I might not be able to find it. I had eleven other people's lives in my hands. If I landed in the wrong spot I could send us all to eternity, plus possibly kill or injure more of the soldiers already on the ground.

I hoped to duplicate my approach and land as close as possible to the spot where I had first landed on the LZ. On short final I searched frantically for the rock. Several of them looked alike. I was about to make a go-around when I spotted the crewchief's discarded, blood-soaked shirt hung up in a bush. Just to the left was the rock. I could now see the crewchief's flight gloves still lying where he had thrown them. The definite imprints of the skids were visible now. The grass was matted down next to the rock.

I lowered the collective and eased the helicopter down. The crewchief was talking me into the skid marks. "A little to the left. Now forward. OK, OK, straight down." We were on the ground in the exact spot.

One of the soldiers with a mine detector stepped out gingerly onto the right skid. He had a head set on and was plugged into the detector. He began sweeping the ground back and forth, stepping forward slowly as he moved the detector before him. The other two men of the team were walking, squatted down and unrolling white ribbon on each side of the cleared path. They were pinning the ribbon in place with nails. The medics were moving cautiously, single file behind the bomb team. They carried their medical supplies and stretchers.

They finally reached the wounded soldier who had lost his hand. He was now lying on his side with his knees still drawn up but was not moving.

The soldier with the mine detector made a complete sweep around the wounded soldier. Satisfied that there were no booby traps nearby, he nodded his head and the medics moved in rapidly and started rendering aid to the unconscious soldier.

The soldier operating the mine detector moved toward the next wounded man.

In what seemed like just a few minutes the medics had the first wounded man bandaged, placed on a stretcher and were carrying him slowly back to the helicopter. After placing him in the helicopter and leaving one medic to attend him, the others made their way back along the path to where the bomb team had just reached the next wounded soldier.

In a short while, the three most seriously wounded soldiers were in the helicopter. The other two wounded were not that serious and it was determined that we should fly out with the three wounded on board and three medics to look after them.

I lifted the helicopter straight up and flew the mile down to the rice paddy. The wounded were transferred to the Dustoff helicopter within a few minutes and were soon on their way to the field hospital.

I flew my helicopter back to the LZ and we repeated the same approach and landing. The last two wounded men were led back to the helicopter. The two medics and four of the other soldiers got on the helicopter and I flew them down to the rice paddy.

I made five more trips back into the booby trapped landing zone. The bomb team had found one more unexploded bomb. It was about twenty-five feet to the right rear of where I had been landing.

The following day I flew the same bomb team, along with Graves and Registration personnel, back into the landing zone to recover the men that had been killed. Out of the four men that had died, there wasn't enough remains to fill one body bag.

Time has helped me forget a lot of the bad moments of Vietnam. Many of the memories have faded away or are stored far away in my mind. Like a dream, you know it was happening to you but you can't quite remember what it was all about.

This situation was different. Although it's been over twenty-two years since that day in May, sometimes whenever I am driving and it begins to rain, the moment I turn the windshield wipers on I feel a momentary grip of terror as the windshield turns briefly into a red blur.

22

The Beasts of Bong Son

It was a night that even the craziest of helicopter pilots, including myself, would have been reluctant to fly around in. It was raining harder than I had ever seen. The rain was hitting the ground with such force that the rain drops were actually bouncing back into the air and then disintegrating into a whitish mist. The mist was thick, resembling a low layer of ground fog.

It was almost eight o'clock and already pitch dark. We had just completed the day's flying. Some of the pilots and helicopters had already departed for Quin Nhon.

The rest of us, about sixteen in all, were going to fly down in two helicopters. There were small arguments as to who would do the flying. No one wanted to trust anyone else to fly in this weather. As short-timers, Owen and I put up a good argument that we should fly. We won out. Owen was the Aircraft Commander of one ship and I of the second helicopter.

There were only two things that would get any of us to fly on a night like this. No one would hesitate to go out after wounded soldiers. The second thing that would entice us out was a party! A party with round-eyed women! Round-eyed nurses! Yeah head for the ships, men!

The nurses at Quin Nhon were moving into new air-conditioned living quarters. They were throwing a house-warming party. They had invited all of the pilots from C Company. They were going to furnish all of the food and booze; we didn't have to bring anything except our bods.

We had gotten to know several of the nurses rather well. A number of them, from time to time, would hop rides on the helicopters and fly back to Bong Son with us on their days off.

One day, as a joke on the infantrymen, I had Lt. Jeanie Butts riding along on a resupply mission. My gunner had checked her out on how to operate the M60 machinegun. Jeanie was riding in the crewchief's seat. She had her hair pushed up under the flight helmet and had the dark sunvisor lowered to conceal her face.

As we landed in the small clearing, the grunts came running out to unload the supplies. Jeanie and the gunner started throwing the boxes into the waiting arms of the soldiers.

I told Jeanie to remove her helmet as if to wipe the perspiration from her forehead.

When she removed the helmet, her pretty brunette hair dropped to her shoulders. Jeanie was a beautiful woman and at first sight of her, all of the soldiers stopped in stunned silence. One soldier let an ammo box he was holding drop onto his foot. He never flinched. Two of the soldiers stood there with sheepish grins, looking like they just happened into the girls locker room.

The gunner hollered, "Let's go. Let's get this shit unloaded," as he threw another box of C-rations. The soldiers began working again but kept their full attention upon Jeanie.

A sergeant jumped up on the skid and shouted through my open window, "Do they allow you guys to have women gunners and crewchiefs?"

"Yeah, Sarg, we're the only outfit to have them," I said. "Because we're the best assault company in Vietnam, they try to keep us happy by giving us anything we want," I lied, trying to keep a straight face.

"Wal, I'll be dipped in buffalo shit," he said, shaking his head and jumping down from the skid.

Several days late our Company Personnel Office received at least a dozen requests for transfers into our company. All were applying for gunner positions.

We lifted off and flew through the heavy rain toward the coast. We followed the coastline south and within an hour were landing at Quin Nhon.

Because of the heavy rains the nurses had decided to have the party at the Officers' Club. Shortly after we arrived, the rains stopped and it was decided to move the party to the courtyard of the new living quarters.

Since we had arrived late and were behind on the drinking, we started drinking the hard booze right from the bottles.

The nurses asked us to help move the food and bottles of liquor to the courtyard. I and two other pilots gathered up six or seven bottles apiece and followed the crowd through a maze of trailers and hootches on the way to the courtyard. Dropping behind in the darkness, we began stashing some of the bottles behind propane tanks and in other available hiding places. We arrived at the courtyard with one bottle apiece. Several of the nurses looked at us suspiciously but never said anything.

We continued to gulp down the liquor and started in on the food. The head nurse, a major, asked us to please stop drinking directly from the bottles and to also use the plates for the food. Some of the pilots were eating potato salad out of the huge bowl using their fingers as a scoop. We laughed at her request, thinking she wasn't serious. This made her mad. The other nurses, doctors and medical personnel were becoming visibly upset, also. Even the nurses that had always been the friendliest toward us were becoming uncomfortable at our roguish behavior.

"I knew it was a mistake to invite these beasts," the major said, loud enough for all to hear. We had heard rumors that they called us the "Beasts of Bong Son" but this was the first time we had actually heard someone say it. Our behavior was always far from being gentlemanly and not becoming of an officer, but we never intentionally did anything to hurt anyone. We had always paid for any damage created by us at their Officers' Club.

The closest we had ever come to creating a real bad disturbance was the night we were all drunk and arguing over who could draw the fastest. Most of the pilots had bought Western–style holsters and fancy gunbelts crammed full of shells for the thirty-eights. The argument became so heated that two of the warrant officers kicked the chairs out of the way and threw the table into the middle of the dance floor. They were facing each other, hands poised above their weapons. The rest of us were backed off to the sides laughing and making bets as to who was fastest.

One of the nurses bravely stepped between the two contestants and got the foolishness stopped. After that, they always had an MP at the door. We had to check our revolvers as we came in.

The statement made by the major ticked us off. Our mood became ugly. Clark, one of the pilots, dropped a glass on the concrete patio, shattering it.

One of the surgeons walked over, grabbed Clark by the shirt and drew back to hit him. Clark tried to explain that the glass had slipped out of his hand and that he was not looking for a fight. The doctor mistook this as a sign of weakness and pursued his blunt aggressiveness. "Maybe some of you other asshole pilots feel lucky," he said, looking around.

"Look, he said he was sorry so why don't you just let it drop," I spoke. I was getting irritated because he still had a hold of Clark's shirt.

"Well, maybe you would like to take his place," the doc said belligerently. He was taller than either Clark or I, but I had no doubt that I could take him out.

"If you want to play badass maybe I will take his place, you cocksucker," I said in a calm voice. I advanced toward him slowly with my arms hanging at my sides. The doc seemed shocked at my abusive language and at calling his bluff.

His hand slowly turned loose of Clark's shirt and came up in a defensive position. "I'll make it easy for you, Doc, I'll let you have the first punch," I said, still advancing with my arms dangling. I had no intention of letting him swing first. From previous experience when I told someone that, one fist or the other would tense up, telling me which arm he was about to throw the punch with. Another quick indication as to whether a person is left or right handed is the wrist he wears his watch on. In almost all cases a person wears his watch on the opposite wrist from the hand he uses most. The doc had his watch on the left wrist. He was right handed. Just as the doc started to tense his right fist, someone grabbed me from behind, pinning my arms at my sides. An impish smile crossed the doc's face as he threw the right hook. I turned my head to the right in order to protect my nose. The punch caught me solidly on the upper part of my left jaw.

"Now you've done it, Doc, I'm pissed off," I said, not feeling any effects from the Sunday punch. First, however, I had to get loose from the fatass captain that still had a bear hug on me. Just as the Doc was getting ready to uncork another haymaker on my jaw, Louie May planted a right jab on Doc's cheek, buckling his knees. This gave me some breathing room and a chance to break loose from Lardo. I twisted my body to one side, flexed my left arm as high as I could and slammed the back of my fist into Lardo's nuts. His arms dropped away like a curtain dropping at the end of a play. The fat captain clutched his groin with both hands. He was bent over and walking aimlessly about the patio. I placed my right hand under his chin and raised his head so I could plant a left on his nose. He looked so pitiful I paused. Aw, I can't punch this poor bastard, I thought. The hell I can't, I argued with myself as I hit him square in the nose. He dropped to his knees still holding his family jewels. Blood trickled from his nose. "Let that be a lesson to ya, fatass," I said, moving off to look for Doc.

By now everyone was into it. Even some of the nurses were clawing at the backs of some of the pilots who were mixing it up with the men of the Medical Corps.

All of the frustrations and tension that had been building up for months were now coming to a climax.

I had always respected the medical people in a combat zone. Their day-to-day lives were always linked to the bloody, broken and mutilated bodies of the wounded. The big difference was that they had to deal with it day in and day out. As pilots, we would fly the wounded to the hospital and then our job was finished.

I was also amazed at the good showing these guys were displaying in this free-for-all. Most of them were young and probably had been athletes in college. They were in good shape.

A warrant officer in fatigues came rushing toward me. I cocked my arm to meet him head on with a left jab. "No! No! I'm on your side," he said. "Who are we fighting?" he asked.

I didn't recognize him. He was from one of the other assault companies of our battalion. He and some other pilots had arrived at the party at the height of the brawl. "Just hit anyone who isn't wearing a 1st Cavalry patch," I told him. I noticed that he didn't have a Cavalry patch on. Hadn't had time to sew it on, I guessed. He melted into the mob and I saw Surf Owen whiz one past his head. He spent more time getting hit by our own people and explaining whose side he was on than he did fighting.

The doc had disappeared. I wanted to plant one on his jaw and return the favor he had done to me.

Louie May and I moved to the long table holding all of the food and beverages. The nurse major was in hysterics.

"Stop it, you filthy animals," she screamed at May and me. Louie grabbed the huge punch bowl and dumped the strawberry colored liquid over the major's head. He then set the upturned bowl down over her head. "There, that ought to cool you down, you old bitch," he said, laughing. She threw the bowl at him, missing his head by inches. The bowl hit the side of one of the new buildings and shattered.

I had moved to the potato salad bowl and was dipping my hands into the potatoes, forming it, like making a snowball, and throwing them at anyone not wearing a Cavalry patch. Unfortunately, I hit Ferdie Wolwhend in the back of the head. The yellow mass clung to his head momentarily and then rolled down his neck, halfway down his back, and then plopped onto the patio floor. Ferdie turned around and gave me a dirty look. I gave him a palms up, "Gee, I'm sorry," shrug and went back to firing the potato balls.

About then a full bird colonel and the doctor that had punched me, came through a sliding glass door.

"What in the hell is going on here?" the colonel shouted. It was obvious the doctor who had started the brawl had gone after the colonel to try and get it stopped.

No one paid any attention to him. None of our guys, anyway. A few medical people had stopped fighting when the colonel shouted, but this caused a couple of them to get clobbered, so they went back to fighting. I whizzed a potato ball past the colonel's head. A small piece of it had broken off during its flight toward the colonel and had splattered onto his glasses.

The screeching whistles drowned out the sounds of the brawl. The MPs came rushing onto the patio with riot clubs held at a ready position. Everyone was about worn out anyway. The brawl stopped abruptly. I reached down and pulled the tablecloth out of the debris scattered about the floor and began wiping the potato salad off my hands.

Most of the nurses stood around the patio sobbing and gazing at the shambles.

"Who started this?" the MP captain wanted to know.

"They did," everyone said, simultaneously pointing their fingers at the opposing force.

"Those vultures did!" the nurse major screeched. She pointed directly at May and me. She was a sight to behold. The punch had soaked her head. Her hair lay matted to her forehead with straggles of it in her eyes.

"I want to know who injured my surgeon's hand," the

colonel chimed in. "Don't you people know these doctors have to operate tomorrow?"

"Gee, Colonel, I bet Sisk is sorry as hell about hitting your surgeon so hard on the fist with his jaw," Surf Owen responded. We all laughed, including some of the medical folks and MPs.

At the mention of my jaw, I felt it with my hand. It was beginning to swell and was becoming painful.

One of the pilots had found a bottle of whiskey that had survived the plunge to the floor and was passing it around. Some of the pilots would take a pull from the bottle, swish it around in their mouths, spit it on the floor and then take another swig and swallow it. This was repulsive to the nurses and they began asking for our removal.

"Who's in charge of you pilots?" the MP captain demanded. We all pointed fingers at each other. Captain May was our ranking officer. "I am. So what?" May asked belligerently.

"I want all of your people's names, rank and what unit you are from," the MP captain continued.

"Fuck you," May replied.

"I'll have to run you guys in if you keep getting smart," the MP said. He was trying to be decent about the whole affair but trying to reason with a bunch of drunks was trying his patience.

"Go ahead and run us in, you prick. Then you can take the responsibility for grounding a whole helicopter assault company. You'll have to explain why we couldn't fly on assaults, extract the men we have in the field already, and cover Medevacs if needed," May rambled on.

The MP captain was undecided as to what to do about us. "OK, if you guys just leave, we'll forget the whole thing," he finally said.

We started shuffling toward the exits. The fat captain that

I had clobbered had found a chair and was sitting dejectedly by himself. One hand still clutched his crotch and the other was holding a handkerchief to his nose.

I couldn't resist. Everyone paused as I walked over to him. "How are you feeling?" I asked in a concerned manner.

"Not very well," he answered, not looking up.

"Take two aspirin and call me in the morning," I said, patting him on the back. Again the pilots roared with laughter.

"Get those bastards out of here," the matted-hair major shouted. We left without responding to the Major's unladylike conduct.

On the way back through the trailers and hootches, we began searching for the bottles of booze we had stashed. We were unable to find one bottle. "Some low-life son-of-a-bitch has stolen all the booze that we stole," a drunken pilot mumbled. "Can't trust no one now-a-days."

Early next morning after only a couple of hours of sleep, we arrived back in Bong Son. The early morning air assault had been called off because of ground fog over the LZ. We had hauled food and supplies out to some of the units and had returned to the mess tent for breakfast. My jaw was so swollen I could not open my mouth far enough to chew any food. The mess sergeant had found a straw for me and I was sipping coffee through it. I was crumbling up crisp bacon and poking it into my mouth, swallowing it without hardly tasting it.

The other pilots sat around toying with their food. Some had black eyes and like me, sore jaws.

Colonel Blair sat at his table, curiously watching us. "What happened to you men, Sisk?" he asked me. I was sitting nearest to him and putting on the weirdest show of trying to eat breakfast. I couldn't move my jaw enough to even talk. He asked Owen. Owen told him about the brawl but made it sound like it was all the medical people's fault. Blair sided with us. "Wish I'd been there. I would have punched their colonel out," he said, angry at the very idea of anyone provoking a fight with his men. A few days later Colonel Blair received a letter condemning our conduct at the party. He tore it up. It was the last we heard about it. We thought that we would be banned from their club in Quin Nhon but we were welcomed as before. We even got along better with the group we had been fighting with.

The nurse major would have nothing to do with us, but she was extremely careful about not using the word *beast*.

23

Countdown to DEROS

"**M**oose bought the farm," Clyde said, walking into our tent. "Plowed into some power lines and crashed into the Saigon River. Killed everyone on board."

Reggie Morse, or Moose as he was called, had been one of our classmates in flight school. Moose had been assigned to Charlie Company the same time I had. Since a large number of us had arrived at the 1st Cavalry about the same time, this meant a large number of us leaving at the same time. They wanted to avoid a large influx of new people so they had transferred a bunch of mid-time pilots out of the Cavalry to other units throughout Vietnam. Their replacements were new guys right out of flight school. By the time the rest of us were ready to leave, the new guys would have several months experience of combat flying.

Moose had been one of the pilots transferred to another aviation company. He had been flying a night mission in bad weather when the accident happened.

He had served in the Army a long time; had fought in Korea as an infantryman and been a sergeant for several years before applying for the Warrant Officer Flight program. His death was a shock to us. No one mentioned Moose after that. It made the rest of us realize that even though we were getting close to going home, we were still in a war and the possibility of getting wounded or killed was still there.

DEROS, pronounced "DEE-ROHS," means, Date of Estimated Return from Overseas. This is one date that anyone who served in Vietnam had etched into their memory. It was the day they were to go home.

When a person became a short timer, he felt obligated to let everyone know about it. I was no different. I taped a piece of plastic on the back of my flight helmet and wrote the number of days left to go on it with a grease pencil. It became a ritual every morning to change the number.

After picking up a load of grunts, we departed Bong Son headed for an air assault in the An Lao Valley. I felt someone tapping me on the shoulder. I turned to find a black soldier grinning and pointing at his helmet. "Short timer," it read. "I've only got twenty-five days to go also, Sir," he shouted above the noise of the helicopter.

I nodded in agreement. "Take care of yourself."

"Oh I will, you can bet on that. This is my last assault and trip to the field. After I do this mission, I go back to the Company H.Q. and just cool it 'til I go home."

I noticed his O.D. name tag on his jungle shirt. Smith, it read. There must be a million Smiths serving in Vietnam, I thought. We had two pilots with that name in my company.

Several days later I was back in the An Lao Valley resupplying the infantry unit we had brought in.

"Can you take two KIA's out?" the lieutenant asked.

"No problem." They loaded the body bags and we headed back to Bong Son. Landing back at LZ English, we shut the helicopter down to await the arrival of the Graves and Registration people. Two other soldiers had flown back in with us. They sat beside the helicopter in silence, smoking cigarettes.

"Poor ole Smitty. Thought he had it dicked," one of the soldiers finally spoke.

"His name is Smith?" I asked.

"Yeah." It couldn't be the Smith I had spoken to a few days ago, I thought. There are just too many Smiths, can't be the same one.

"Yep, Smitty only had twenty-two days to go. Was supposed to go back to base camp tomorrow," he added.

It was the same guy. Now I wished I'd never spoken to the soldier about being a short timer. I felt terrible about his death. I didn't ask about how he was killed. I didn't want to know.

A few days later a gunship was shot down in the An Lao Valley killing all four crew members. Every one of them had less than a month to go before they went home.

I began to worry a little about it. I had less than twenty days to go. When I first arrived in the Cavalry, they would let the short timers go back to An Khe, our base camp, two weeks early. Then they cut it down to one week and then we found out that we would fly combat missions right up to two days before we were due to go home.

For eleven months I had been involved and exposed to violent death and destruction. The first month in the country was frightening, but later all the flying and action seemed almost routine. Even the night missions didn't seem to bother me.

But now, into my last month before DEROS, I was feeling the same apprehension and concern that I had the first month in Vietnam.

I was determined to do my job and not let myself get paranoid over this danger to short timers. The An Lao Valley and the triple canopy jungle mountains surrounding the valley seemed to bother me the most. I guess because it was where most of our flying and firefights were taking place.

In the last several weeks, several close calls to myself and the other airmen of Charlie Company, 229th A.H.B., had taken place in the An Lao area.

"Rittman's helicopter is grounded. Have your crew help Rittman's crew transfer the ammo and other supplies from his ship to yours," the operations officer told me.

I walked to the top of the little hill where the helicopters were parked. My gunner and crewchief were already busy packing the crates of ammo from Rittman's helicopter to ours. Rittman and his co-pilot were standing beside their helicopter counting bullet holes. The right side of the helicopter was riddled with holes.

"What in the hell happened?" I asked.

"We made three tries at getting this stuff into the LZ and got the shit shot out of us each time, Rittman answered. "Are you going to fly this stuff in?"

"Yeah, I guess so. Operations didn't say anything about you guys getting shot up. I figured your helicopter just broke down," I said.

Rittman briefed me on the location of the LZ and where the enemy fire was coming from. The LZ was located on a finger ridge on the west side of the An Lao Valley. The enemy fire was coming from another ridge northwest of the LZ.

We crested the line of mountains separating the An Lao Valley from the Bong Son Plain. I made radio contact with the infantry unit we were to resupply.

"We're still receiving sporadic fire from that ridgeline," the radio operator informed me. "Winds are out of the west at about 10 knots."

Rittman had told me that the best approach to the LZ was from the east. To approach from the west would require coming down the ridge line at a very steep descent, which would require a slow approach. This would be asking for trouble. The wind was favorable for the east to west approach. I told the crewchief and gunner to test fire their machineguns. Both M60s rattled a short burst simultaneously.

"Pop smoke so I can pinpoint your location. I'm ready to come in," I radioed the men on the landing zone.

"OK, I've got orange smoke."

"Roger, orange smoke," the radio operator confirmed.

I began the approach from the east while still over the valley floor. Since the LZ was high on the finger ridge I was already at the same altitude. My plan was to make a fairly fast, straight-in approach to the landing zone.

At about one hundred yards from the LZ, tracer rounds began spewing from the dense dark foliage on the ridge to our northwest. I could follow the stream of tracers and watched them streak harmlessly by several yards in front of the helicopter. The Bad Guys were leading us too much.

I suddenly thought back to my duck hunting days on the Illinois River and all the ducks I missed by doing the same thing. What a stupid damn thing to be thinking about at a time like this. Get your head out of your ass, Sisk, I thought.

"Heavy fire from our right front," the gunner said,

breaking the silence over the intercom. About the same time the radio operator broke in over the Fox Mike radio. "Charlie has opened up again. Have you got the fire, White Two?" he asked.

"Roger that," I replied. I could see what the bastards had in mind. They already had the range on the spot where we would be landing. They were simply going to lead the fire right to the LZ and continue to fire into the touchdown spot while we flew directly into it.

I jammed the cyclic control to the right and rolled the helicopter over into a steep descending right turn. We leveled out above the drainage between the ridges and flew low level back to the valley. Reaching the safety of the valley we climbed to two thousand feet and began an orbit.

"White Two, thanks for trying anyway," the radio operator said.

"We haven't given up yet. We're going to try and figure out something else," I replied. I told the co-pilot to take the controls. I pulled the Code and Radio Frequency Book from the pocket of my chicken plate or chest protector. I found the UHF frequency for the Forward Air Controller assigned to the 1st Cavalry, based at Bong Son. I was hoping that the small Air Force spotter plane might be in the area. I turned in the frequency.

"Whiplash, are you up on this freq.?"

I received an immediate answer. "Roger. Who's calling?" replied Whiplash.

"This is Wagonwheel White Two. We've got a little problem over here in the An Lao. We are trying to get some ammo in to a unit that is pinned down. We don't have any gunships available and I was wondering if you had anything available?" I asked.

"Stand by, White Two, I'll see what we have in the area."

A few minutes later Whiplash called back. "White Two, I've got a couple of 100's about a hundred and fifty miles north. They aborted their mission and are looking for a place to unload. I can have them down here in ten to fifteen minutes."

"OK, bring them down. I'll advise the ground units as to what we are going to do," I said. I gave Whiplash the coordinates of the LZ and the location of the enemy unit and then called the infantry unit on the LZ and told them of the planned air strike.

In about twelve minutes the F-100's were orbiting over the valley. "I'll have our ground unit mark their location with smoke and then I'll mark the enemy location with a couple of 'Willie Peter' Rockets," the air controller told the F-100 pilots.

The F-100's began their runs on the ridge line occupied by the enemy. The jungle was burning fiercely from the napalm. The 100's then strafed the area and pulled up several thousand feet above the valley floor. "We are running low on fuel and have to return to base. Hope we did some good for you," the flight leader of the F-100's told the FAC.

"Roger that. Thanks for the help. I'll buy you guys a beer some night," Whiplash responded.

As before, I started the approach to the landing zone from the east. This time on short final we didn't see any tracer rounds. Touching down in the small clearing, the crewchief and some of the infantry men began throwing the ammo and other supplies out of the helicopter. The gunner sat with his machinegun pointed toward the ridge line. Just as the last boxes were being unloaded, the infantrymen suddenly dived behind the downed logs lying around the landing spot. About the same time Brown opened up with the M60. Tracers from his machinegun disappeared into the foliage on the far ridge. A bullet slammed into a log directly in front of the helicopter sending splinters of wood flying.

Johnson kicked the last boxes out the door as I was lifting the helicopter off the landing zone. This time I dove the helicopter to the left seeking safety on the back side of the ridge. In a matter of seconds we were below the ridge and out of line of the enemy fire.

The Air Force had knocked out the machineguns allowing us to get the ammo into the LZ. Some of the enemy soldiers had survived the air strike, however, and were able to fire a few harassment shots at us. None of the soldiers or the aircraft was hit. I thanked Whiplash for his help and we returned to Bong Son.

After shutting down the helicopter, I couldn't wait to have this day over with. I grabbed my grease pencil and changed the number of days left on my flight helmet. It seemed to help.

24

The Freedom Bird

It was still pitch dark. I hadn't slept very well during the night, but I was anxious to get up and more than a little excited. I flipped my sleeping bag open and grappled in the dark for my flashlight. Having found it, I shined it on my watch. 0400. I could stay in my sleeping bag a little longer but I knew I wouldn't be able to sleep. Next to going home it was the day I had been looking forward to. It was the sixteenth day of July, Nineteen sixty-seven.

Following the same routine I had been practicing for the last year, I checked each leg of my jungle fatigue pants closely for scorpions and snakes. Satisfied, I slid the trousers on. Still not touching my bare feet on the ammo box floor. Holding the flashlight with one hand I reached down and shook each sock vigorously and then each boot. Only after each boot was on and fully laced did I put my feet on the floor and stand up.

I finished dressing in silence, not wanting to wake or disturb the other seven pilots I shared the tent with. Strapping my gunbelt and survival knife on, I headed for the mess tent. It was too early for breakfast but I wouldn't be able to eat anyway. The coffee would be ready; that's what I needed.

Several of the cooks were relaxing at one of the tables as I entered the mess tent. I poured myself a cup of coffee and joined the cooks at their table.

"What are you doing up so early, Mr. Sisk?" asked the mess sergeant.

"Today is my last day of combat assaults. Tomorrow I go back to An Khe for two days and then it's the land of the big PX," I bragged. "I guess I'm just anxious to get it over with".

The mess sergeant and cooks expressed their genuine happiness for me. I suddenly felt a little bit ashamed about the bragging, knowing that these guys still had time to serve in Vietnam. I changed the subject.

0530. We departed the Bong Son for an air assault in the hills north of the Bong Son Plain. Thank God we're not going into the An Lao, I thought. "Maybe I'll have an easy day and get this over with."

The air assault was almost letter perfect. The landing zone was prepped by artillery and aerial artillery helicopters. All eight of our helicopters landed simultaneously while Delta Company gunships strafed the brush and tree line surrounding the landing zone. No enemy fire was detected. We returned to Bong Son to pick up the troopers for the second wave into the same landing zone. After dropping off the second load of infantry, we returned to LZ English. About half way through our breakfast, the operations sergeant burst through the mess tent door.

"They want those guys we just put into the LZ extracted," he shouted. Everyone scrambled for the tent opening. We ran for the helicopters. My crewchief and gunner were already at the helicopter untying the blades. Everyone was wondering what was happening.

The helicopters lifted off and joined up in formation. We flew at maximum speed toward the LZ. We began to outdistance the heavily ladened gunships. The flight leader slowed the air speed slightly to allow the B-model Huey gunships to catch up.

The Battalion CO, orbiting the LZ in the Charlie-Charlie ship, briefed us on the situation over the UHF radio.

It appeared that we had put our troops into an area that contained several companies of North Vietnamese regulars. The NVA had waited until all the helicopters had departed and then attacked our out-numbered troops, driving them back to the LZ. There were no available forces to reinforce our troops. The Ready Reaction Force usually used for such occasions had already been committed to another battle in a different area.

The decision was made to extract our troops and use air power to destroy the enemy force.

Alpha Company of the 229th Assault Helicopter Battalion was on the way to extract troopers from another area. They were diverted to our landing zone to help get two lifts of soldiers out.

Both flights arrived at the LZ about the same time. Artillery from a nearby firebase had been pounding the area around the landing zone. The artillery fire was halted to let the helicopters get in to make the extraction. Several ARA ships had arrived and were now rocketing the tree lines bordering the landing zone.

The LZ would only hold eight helicopters at a time. It

was decided that Alpha Company would go in first. We would follow and make the final lift.

Our soldiers were lying inside the LZ, several yards from the tree line. The NVA had managed to encircle the landing zone and were firing from all sides. The gunship escorts from our flight and from Alpha Flight had joined with the AA helicopters and were in a daisy chain orbit on both sides of the landing zone, pouring a continuous rain of rocket and machinegun fire into the tree lines. The eight helicopters of Alpha Company touched down on the LZ in trail formation. The soldiers going out on the first lift ran in a low crouch toward the helicopters. Several of the soldiers were dragging their wounded buddies. In a matter of seconds the helicopters were loaded and lifting out of the LZ.

Our flight was on short final. Our gunners were lacing the tree line, a solid stream of tracers spewing from the guns. They stopped firing as we touched down in order to let our soldiers get to the helicopters. The soldiers were backing away from the tree lines, firing their weapons as they went. Again the wounded were being pulled and carried toward the ships. Now some of the braver NVA were running out into the open and firing on the helicopters. A soldier helping a wounded friend, went down. Another stopped, attempting to help both downed men. A gunner from the ship in front of me leaped from the helicopter and ran to the aid of the three men. Together they made it to the helicopter.

"White Four, are we up?" Yellow One, our flight leader, asked.

"Negative, Sir. They're still trying to get some of the wounded loaded," White Four replied. We could not lift out of the LZ until we were certain we had everyone on board. To leave anyone would mean certain death for them.

The last of the soldiers were getting on the helicopters.

Our gunners had opened up with their machineguns again, knocking several of the NVA to the ground.

"Flight is up," the aircraft commander of White Four shouted over the radio.

"Runaway rocket," another voice broke in. "It's going into the LZ," the gunship pilot shouted in a panicky voice. The fins on the tail of the rocket had failed too open or had broken off, sending the rocket out of control. It exploded thirty feet to my left, showering my door window and the left side of the helicopter with mud, debris and shrapnel.

"Wagonwheel flight lifting," our flight leader said. All eight helicopters lifted and accelerated up and out of the LZ. The NVA swarmed into the LZ, firing up at us. Our gunners continued pouring fire back at them.

I scanned my instruments for any indication of trouble. Everything seemed normal. "Johnson, give me an assessment of damage from that rocket," I asked.

"One of the grunts got hit in the mouth with a rock or something. He's got a bloody lip but seems all right. I got a face full of mud from the explosion but everything else appears to be OK," Johnson answered.

We returned to Bong Son. The helicopters with wounded aboard dropped the men off at the field hospital. After shutting down, we checked the helicopter for further damage. We found one bullet hole in one of the main rotor blades and another bullet had smashed into the bulkhead just to the right of where Brown, the gunner, was sitting. It continued through the bulkhead into the fuel cell. From the angle it had entered, the bullet had missed Brown's head by only a few inches. Out of the sixteen helicopters participating in the extraction, only a few had gone unscathed.

Owen, Bair, Clyde and myself were all due to leave for An Khe. All of us had been on the extraction. It was a very close call for us. During our twelve months in 'Nam, Owen and Bair had been shot down, Clyde had been shot. I felt very lucky. I patted the little Testament tucked in the left breast pocket of my jungle shirt. My mother had given it to me in nineteen forty-eight. I wasn't a very religious person but I had carried the Testament on every combat mission. Over a thousand flying hours over Vietnam.

Early the next morning I made the rounds saying my goodbyes to the other pilots, my crewchief and gunner.

Bair and I flew a helicopter back to An Khe, making a low-level pass over the company area prior to departing Bong Son.

After arriving back at An Khe, I spent most of the day straightening out my uniforms and processing out of Charlie Company. My next duty assignment was to be an Aviation Unit in Thailand. Most of my belongings would be shipped directly to Korat. I would be taking a month's leave back in the States. I was only going to take a minimum amount of uniforms with me.

That night, we all gathered at the 229th Battalion Officers' Club for a farewell party. Most of us that were going home had been in the same class in flight school. Some of our classmates from other units showed up. Brian Pray, from Charlie Company, 227th Assault Helicopter Battalion, arrived. I had run across Pray several times during the year in Vietnam. The last time, several months before, in Quin Nhon. We had been drinking in the Officers' club and decided to contact Springer. Telling the military operator that he was a full colonel and it was a top priority call, Pray finally contacted Springer. He was at a base forty miles west of Quin Nhon. Pray and I told him we'd be over to pick him up. We went out to the airfield and stole the first Huey we came to. We flew in the dark and heavy rains to the base, picked Springer up and returned to partying at Quin Nhon, all in an hour's time.

Again I awoke early. This was it. The last day in Vietnam. Even with the hangover from the party the previous night, I felt great.

A company clerk drove us to the airstrip. Several C-130's sat on the ramp. I couldn't believe the number of soldiers lined up waiting to board the airplanes.

We joined a cluster of pilots that were laughing and clowning around. Most of them had been at the party at the Officers' Club. Like me, they had hangovers but nothing could spoil this day.

They started reading off names and the soldiers began loading into the C-130's. I was called to board the third aircraft. Bair, Clyde, Owen and Pray had boarded the second 130. We had decided to have a party at a certain hotel in San Francisco. We had planned the party at the Officers' Club the night before, knowing we might be separated on the flights out of Vietnam.

We were to ride the 130's to Pleiku and then transfer to the huge C-141 troop transports. The "Freedom Bird" as it became known. It was the reverse trip of the way I had arrived a year earlier. The only difference was that we were riding the four-engine C-130's to Pleiku instead of the twin engine Caribou that had brought us to An Khe.

I plopped into one of the canvas troop seats and fastened my seat belt. They kept crowding the soldiers on. All the seats were full and soldiers began filling the center passageway separating the two rows of jump seats. I was becoming very nervous over this whole deal. About ten months earlier, a C-130 loaded to the gills, had aborted its takeoff, ran off the end of the runway and burst into flames killing over thirty GI's on their way home.

Finally they raised the rear ramp, rolling the last of the soldiers down on top of the men sitting at the rear of the airplane. "A hell of a way to treat people that have just spent a year in a shit bowl,'' I said to the captain sitting next to me.

The C-130 taxied slowly out to the runway. After lining up on the runway, the engines roared to take off power. The pilot was still holding the brakes. The airplane squatted on its nose wheel while the whole aircraft strained and shuddered against the locked tires. Finally the pilot released the brakes and the C-130 leaped forward. I said a silent prayer, looked around and spotted the nearest exit, planning my escape route.

We were finally airborne. The last part of the "golf course," the world's largest heliport, disappeared under the 130's belly. "Thank you, Lord. We're getting this done little by little," I whispered.

In what seemed like just a few minutes, we were breaking out of the low-hanging clouds and landing at Pleiku.

After taxiing to the ramp, we off-loaded and reassembled to be manifested on a C-141. As we were taxiing in, a 141 had taken off. I couldn't see any other 141's anywhere. I was concerned about spending another night in Vietnam. I couldn't see any of my friends or anyone I knew. They had all made it out on the earlier C-141.

"Damn it to hell," I swore. No sooner had I spoken than another 141 broke out of the clouds and landed.

"You men will be boarding this aircraft after it has off loaded its passengers," a sergeant with a bullhorn announced.

The door on the airplane opened. The newly arrived soldiers filed off the plane in silence. It seemed like only yesterday that I had walked off an airplane in this very same place. We stood there silently, patiently waiting to take these men's seats. I stared at their faces. Most looked around, bewildered. Some appeared outright frightened. I wondered how many would never return alive. I felt sorry for them knowing what they had in store for them.

Soldiers from our group began filing onto the airplane. They called my name, I trotted to the line and shuffled with the other men toward the door. Just before I stepped into the aircraft, I took one final look around. Helicopters were lifting off on the other side of the airfield. I could see the infantrymen, some of them with their legs dangling out of the open doors, their weapons lying on their laps. I could hear artillery off in the distance. The war was still going on. Had the year I spent here helped or contributed in any manner? I didn't know.

After what seemed like an eternity, the Air Force crewmen shut and secured the door. I tightened my seat belt another notch. Unlike the C-130, the seats on this airplane were the airline type and fairly comfortable. The jet engines were started and then the airplane began to taxi slowly toward the runway. Everyone sat completely motionless and in silence. A soldier across the aisle coughed. Heads turned silently, scowling at the man that had coughed. No one wanted anything to happen that would jeopardize our leaving. The soldier stared at his feet, his hand held over his mouth.

The airplane made a turn and stopped. The four jet engines built to one huge roar. The C-141 began rolling, picking up speed by the second. It pitched up into a climb attitude. The sound of the landing gear being retracted could be heard above the engine's noise. In seconds the huge airplane popped into the safety of the low-hanging clouds. As if on cue, an enormous roar erupted from the soldiers. It had happened. The Freedom Bird had freed us from this place. We were going home.

ABOUT THE AUTHOR

Robert W. Sisk presently works as a contract pilot.

He first learned to fly fixed-wing aircraft in 1962. In 1965 Sisk enlisted in the U.S. Army under the Warrant Officer Flight Training Program.

After graduation from rotary-wing flight school, he served two years in Southeast Asia, accumulating over 1,800 flying hours.

His first year was spent flying assault helicopters with the 1st Air Cavalry. He was awarded the Distinguished Flying Cross, the Bronze Star and 23 air medals.

His last assignment in the Army was as a test pilot for weapon systems on helicopters.